Targeting PHONICS

★ Book 2 ★

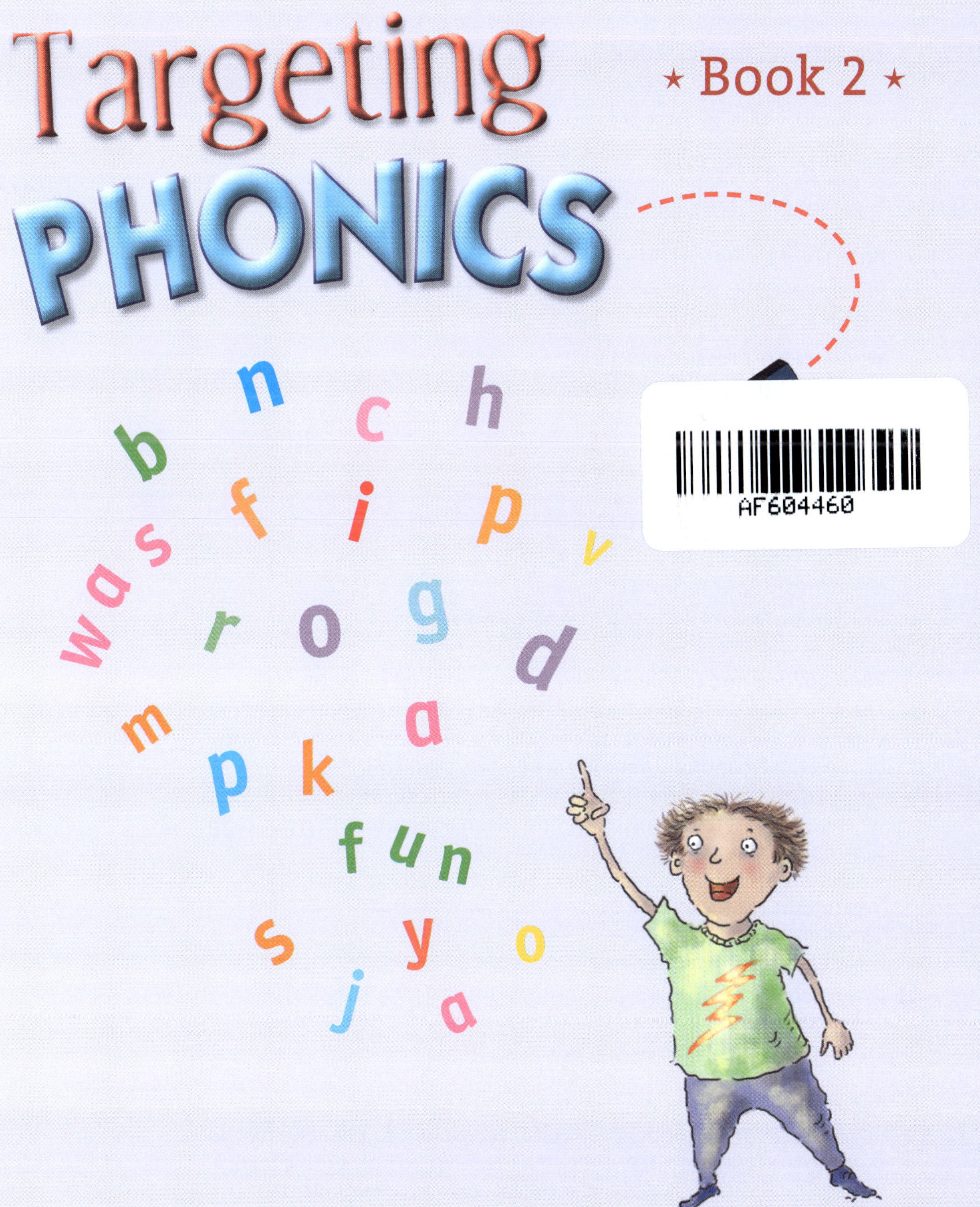

This book belongs to

....

....

Targeting Phonics Book 2

Reprinted 2023, 2026

ISBN: 978-1-92572-635-0

Published by Pascal Press
PO Box 250
Glebe NSW 2037
www.pascalpress.com.au
contact@pascalpress.com.au

Design: Janice Bowles
Author: Norah Colvin
Publisher: Lynn Dickinson
Typesetter: BSMART Publishing
Illustrator: Paul Lennon
Printed by Vivar Printing/Green Giant Press

⋆ Contents ⋆

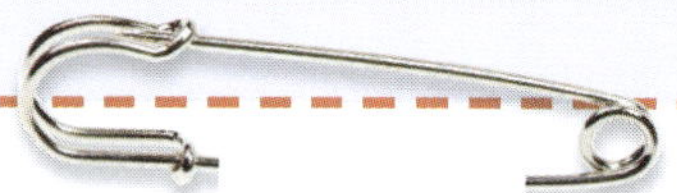

⋆ Phonics explained ⋆

Phonics helps children decode words for reading
and encode words for spelling.

Decoding requires them to see the letters, match them with a sound and blend the sounds together to say the word.

Encoding requires them to hear the sounds in a word and match each sound with a corresponding letter or combination of letters.

The ability to decode and encode words efficiently underpins success with reading and writing.

The *Targeting Phonics* series uses a systematic ***synthetic phonics*** approach with reference to the progression recommended in the Australian Curriculum. It introduces students to the 26 letters of the alphabet (*graphemes*) and their relationship to the 44 sounds (*phonemes*) of the English language, which the letters represent.

The ***synthetic phonics*** approach encourages children to listen to all the phonemes (individual sounds) and blend or 'synthesise' them to form words, such as 'b' + 'a' + 't' = bat. Reading and spelling are taught in relationship to each other — if you can read a word, you can spell it. Writing the words also helps to consolidate this learning and is included in every unit.

Prior to the synthetic phonics methodology, schools often used ***analytic phonics***, where children were encouraged to identify the sound of the first letter and guess the rest of the word using rhymes or word-building strategies such as onset and rime. Reading and spelling were taught as separate skills, rather than being integrated.

⋆ About the author ⋆

Norah Colvin is a teacher with over 20 years' experience in early childhood classrooms. She is passionate about literacy education and enjoys sharing children's first steps into literacy. She has also supported learners who experienced difficulty attaining literacy skills the first time round.

⋆ How to use this book ⋆

In Book 2 students are introduced to the following after a brief review on pages 2-5 of Book 1:

- the long vowel sounds a, e, i, o and u, and different ways of spelling them
- the consonant digraphs sh, ch, th (voiced and unvoiced), ph, ng and wh
- about using the letters c and k when spelling words with the hard c sound
- about the soft c and soft g sounds
- that the digraph oo can be used to represent both a long vowel sound and a short vowel sound
- that the letter s can be used to represent different sounds.

Each sound is introduced with photographic Sound Cards of four things that contain the sound. These cards can be accessed online via the QR code on the same page where they will hear the correct pronunciation of the sound. Students should watch and listen to the sound card before completing the corresponding activities.

At the completion of each unit, students read, spell and blend words formed using the new sounds in combination with those previously learned.

Revision of known letters and sounds is included in each unit with a full assessment of all units at the end of the book.

Read and Spell

As students' knowledge of the ways individual letters and digraphs (graphemes) are used to represent sounds, they learn to read and spell an increasing number of decodable words by blending the graphemes to form CV, VC, CVC, CCVC, CVCC words. Note: *C=consonant, V= vowel*

Students read sentences formed from a combination of those decodable words and a small number of high frequency words introduced in each unit.

Students spell decodable words by stretching out the sounds in CV, VC, CVC, CCVC, CVCC words formed from known graphemes.

High Frequency Words

Students learn to recognise by sight a number of high frequency words in each unit. Lists of high frequency words are included in the back of the book.

Comprehension

Students read short paragraphs formed using decodable and known high frequency words to practise reading and comprehension skills.

It is suggested that students proceed through the book, completing the lessons in sequence, to ensure that all words encountered in activities have already been learned, either as decodable words or high frequency words.

★ Glossary ★

Analytic phonics	starts with a word and takes it apart to identify its parts, *for example: 'bat' = 'b' + 'at'*
Consonants	are produced when the air is restricted in some way; in English there are 24 consonant sounds, most of which are represented by one letter and some which are represented by two letters, such as 'sh' and 'ch'
Decode	see the letters, match them with a sound and blend the sounds together to say the word
Digraph	a combination of two letters representing one sound, *for example: 'sh' as in 'shoe', 'ch' as in 'church', 'th' as in 'thimble' or 'there', 'oa' as in 'boat' or 'ea' as in 'peach'*
Encode	listen to the sounds in a word and write the corresponding letter or combination of letters to match each sound
Graphemes	letters used to represent the sounds of the language
Long vowels	vowel sounds that are long in duration
Phonemes	individual units of sound heard in the language
Phonics	the relationships between graphemes and phonemes; understanding how letters and groups of letters are used to represent the sounds of the language
Phonemic awareness	the ability to hear and manipulate different sounds in words
Short vowels	vowel sounds that are short in duration and cannot be lengthened without distortion
Split digraph	when the two letters that represent one sound are split by another letter, *for example: ae as in 'cake'*
Synthetic phonics	starts with individual sounds and blends them together to form words, *for example: 'b' + 'a' + 't' = 'bat'*
Trigraphs	three letters used to represent one sound, *for example: 'igh' as in 'high' or 'light'*
Quadgraphs	four letters used to represent one sound, *for example: 'eigh' as in 'eight' or 'weight'*
unvoiced consonants	consonants that are made without vibrating the vocal cords
voiced consonants	consonants that are made using the vocal cords
Vowels	sounds formed without obstruction to the flow of air by the tongue, teeth or lips; usually represented by the letters 'a', 'e', 'i', 'o', and 'u', either individually or in combination; the letters are sometimes combined with 'y' as in 'boy' or 'w' as in 'cow'; a vowel is usually necessary in every word and syllable in the English language

★ Version 9.0 Australian Curriculum correlations ★

Targeting Phonics Book 2 teaches students the common long vowel sounds and common consonant digraphs. In addition, students will:

- Segment words into separate phonemes (sounds) including consonant blends or clusters at the beginnings and ends of words (phonological awareness) (AC9E1LY09)
- Use short vowels, common long vowels, consonant blends and digraphs to write words, and blend these to read one- and two-syllable words (AC9E1LY11)
- Understand that a letter can represent more than one sound and that a syllable must contain a vowel sound (AC9E1LY12)
- Read decodable and authentic texts using developing phonic knowledge, phrasing and fluency, and monitoring meaning using context and grammatical knowledge (AC9E1LY04)
- Spell one- and two-syllable words with common letter patterns (AC9E1LY13)
- Read and write an increasing number of high frequency words (AC9E1LY14)
- Write words using unjoined lower-case and upper-case letters (AC9E1LY08)

⋆ Games to teach decoding & encoding skills ⋆

Games provide students with fun opportunities to practise their decoding skills and to reinforce their recognition of high frequency words.

⋆ Pick Two ⋆

You need: Word Cards from the back of the book, cut and laminated for durability.

How to play:

1. Spread the cards out, face down, on the table.
2. Children take turns to choose two cards. They read the words and make a sentence using them. It can be sensible, silly or funny.
3. Children keep the words they selected if they were decoded and used in sentence correctly.

Extension:

1. Pencil and paper required.
2. One child repeats the two words, and the other children write them. The words are then shown. Children check if they are spelled correctly.
3. When all the words are used, children count the number of words spelled correctly. They make a learning list of those that are not correct.

⋆ Thingamajig — What's it called ⋆

You need: the target sound, one of the vowel or consonant sounds learned in the book. Write it on a card, for example: sh.

How to play:

1. Point to any object in the room, for example a book or a vase. This object is a decoy. It doesn't have the target sound.
2. Children take turns to point to the decoy object and say a word that contains the target sound; for example, they might say, 'shoe', 'shell', 'shamrock', 'shelter' or 'shape'.
3. Children are out if they say the name of the decoy object or can't think of a word with the target sound. They must not repeat a word already suggested.
4. The game continues until only one player is left or no more words are suggested.

⋆ Games to teach high frequency words ⋆

⋆ Your choice bingo ⋆

You need: Word Cards from the back of the book, cut and laminated for durability. A pencil and a sheet of A4 paper for each child. Fold the paper in half along the long edge, and then again. Then fold it in half from end to end. There should be eight boxes when unfolded.

How to play:

1. Place the words face up on the table.
2. Each child chooses eight words and writes them onto their bingo sheet, one per box.
3. Turn over and shuffle the word cards.
4. Call each word and children colour the box if they have it on their sheet.
5. First to complete their sheet is the winner and yells 'Bingo!'.

⋆ Bucket ⋆

You need: Word cards from the back of the book, photocopied, cut and laminated. Four similar cards with the word bucket written on them.

How to play:

1. Place all the word cards, including bucket cards, into a small bucket.
2. Children take turns to take a word from the bucket. If they can read the word they keep it. Then it is the next child's turn. If they take the word bucket, they must place all their words back into the bucket. The word bucket is then put aside.
3. The winner is the child with the most words when no words remain in the bucket. Because the game involves a certain amount of luck as well as recognising words, everyone has a chance of winning.

⋆ Revision of Book 1 ⋆

In Book 1, we learned all letters of the alphabet and their most common sounds. This includes the 21 consonants and 5 short vowel sounds. We blended the sounds to read words and listened to sounds in words to spell them. We also learned some high frequency words.

The following exercises provide practise with what was learned in Book 1 before we go on to new work.

Decoding

Read the words. Draw lines to match them to the pictures.

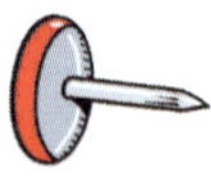	map		fox		zip
	hut	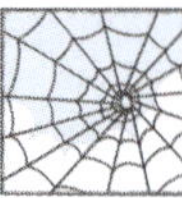	cap		doll
	pin		web		bus

Spelling

Say the names of the pictures below. Stretch out the word to hear the sound at the beginning, middle and end. Write the words on the lines below.

Spelling

Choose letters you know to complete these words. Read the words.

s____t   ca____   h____m

____ill   be____   ____ack

____en   do____   d____mp

High frequency words

In Book 1, you learned these high frequency words.
Colour the words you know. Practise the ones you need to learn.

I	a	the	this	is
see	good	away	boy	on
here	look	that	he	my
has	have	to	said	like
you	me	are	go	down
girl	too	with	little	come
we	no	where	some	going
was	mother	father	they	into

  ISBN: 9781925726350

Comprehension

Read the sentences. Draw a picture to match.

A big red truck was going up the hill. A little black car was going down the hill. They met at the well.	The pig was in the mud. The duck sat on a log. The duck fell in the mud. It said, 'Quack!'

I have a pet dog. The boy has a pet cat. The girl has a pet pig. We like the pets. They are fun.	Mother was in the tent. A crab went in the tent. "No," said Mother. "A crab in the tent is not good. Go away, crab!"

  ISBN: 9781925726350

Comprehension

Look at the pictures. Read the sentences. Write in the missing word.

The boy has a cut ___ ___ ___ ___.
He cut it on a rock.

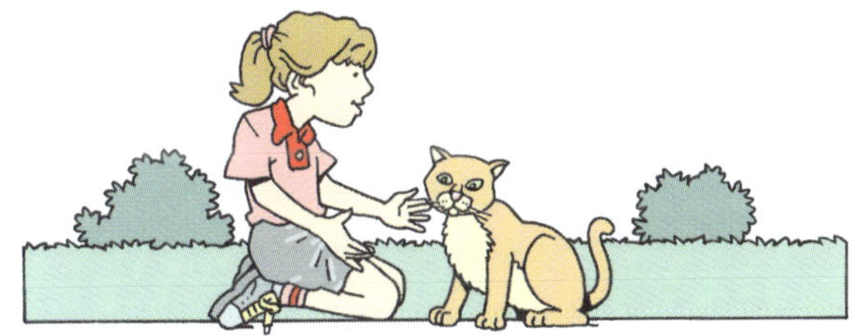

I can see a girl with a little pet ___ ___ ___.

Look at the little ___ ___ ___ ___ in the big ___ ___ ___ truck.

This sentence is jumbled. Write it correctly on the lines below.

went Dan in Sam van. and black a

  ISBN: 9781925726350

Long vowel sound a with split digraph a_e as in *cake*

Use this QR code to watch and listen to the **letter A_E** sound cards below

 cake	 plane
 cape	 gate

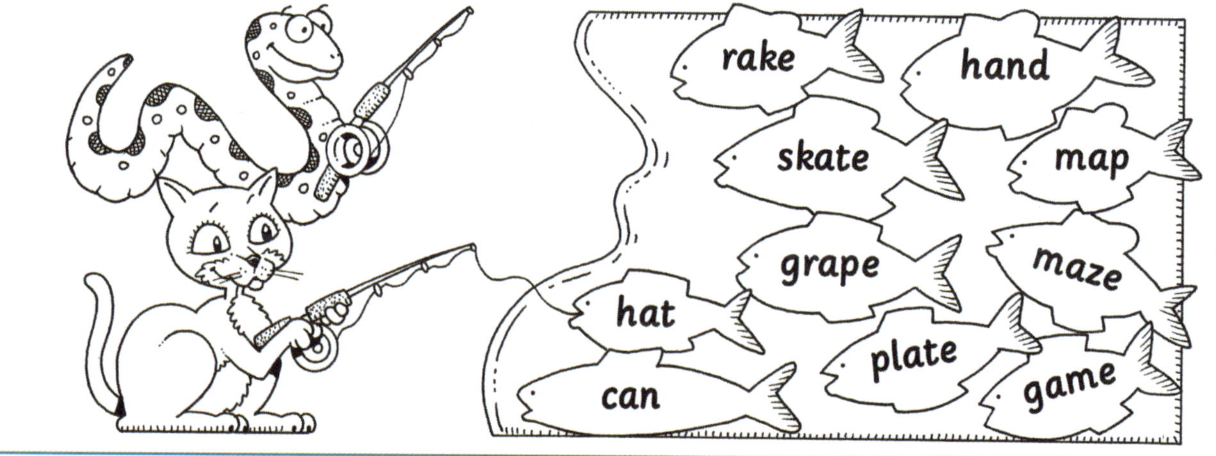

Help them catch their favourite fish by drawing red lines to the short **a** words and blue lines to the long **a** words.

  ISBN: 9781925726350

Long vowel sound a with split digraph a_e as in *cake*

Say the names of the pictures. Write the word below.
Don't forget the 'e' on the end.

Handwriting

Trace the words then copy them onto the lines below.

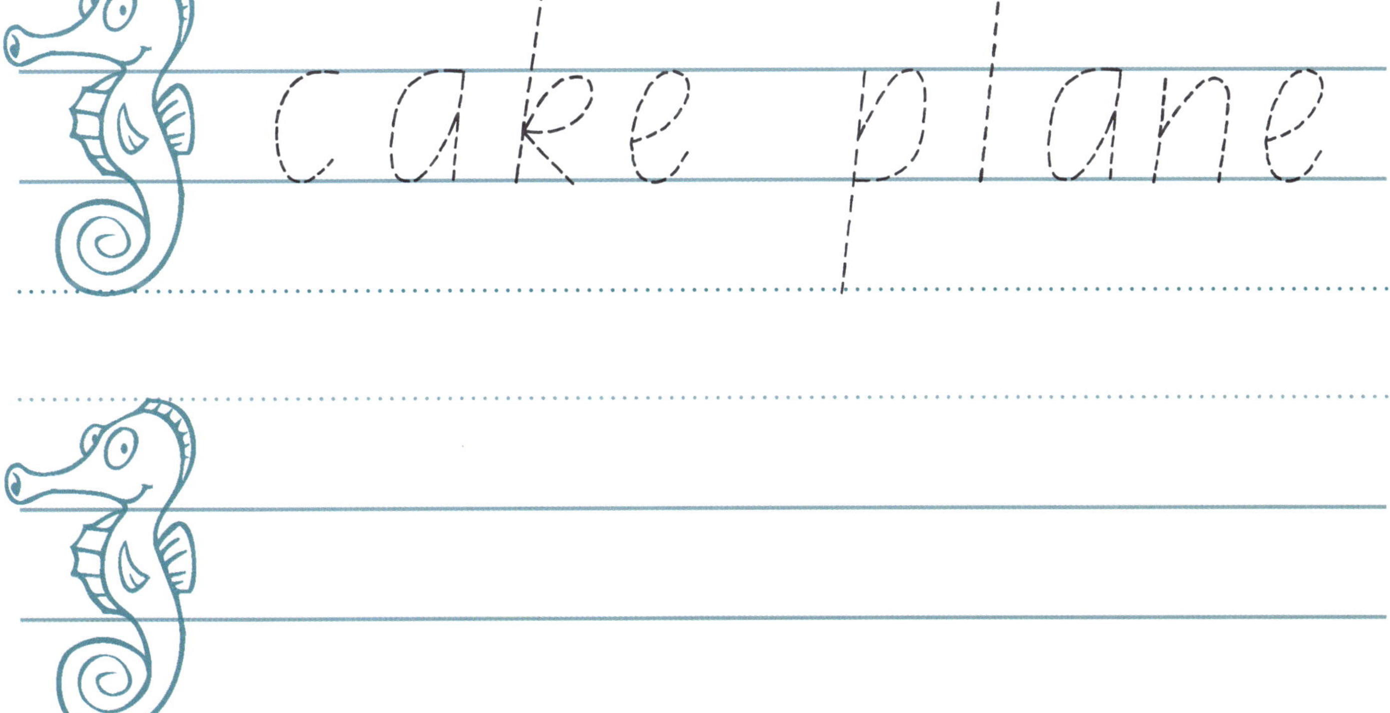

  ISBN: 9781925726350

Consonant sound sh with the digraph sh as in *shop*

sh

Use this QR code to watch and listen to the **letter SH** sound cards below

 shop	 ship
 fish	 dish

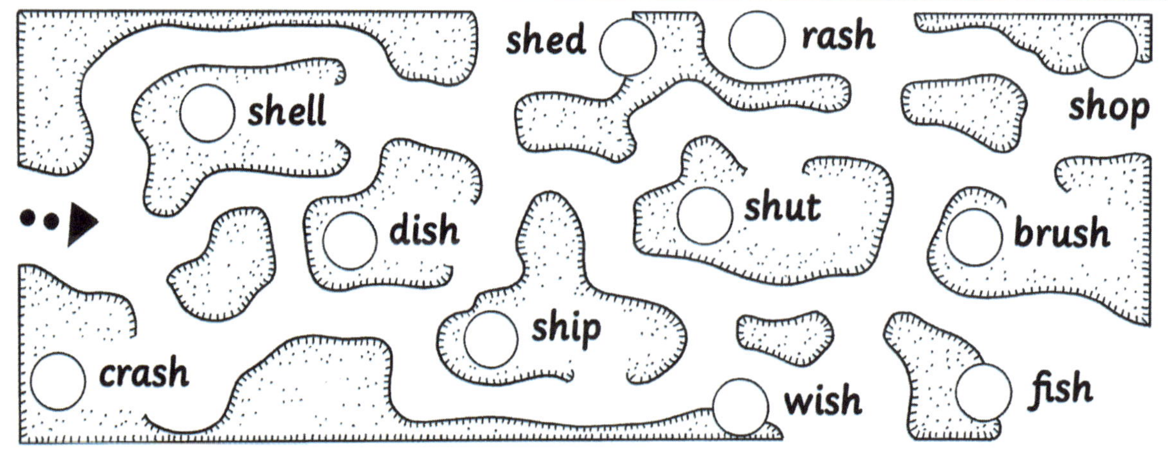

Write **b** in the circles for words beginning with **sh** and **e** if the word ends in **sh**.

  ISBN: 9781925726350

Consonant sound sh with the digraph sh as in *shop*

Say the names of the pictures. Listen for the 'sh' sound. Write the word below.

Handwriting

Trace the words then copy them onto the lines below.

  ISBN: 9781925726350

Long vowel sound  with split digraph i_e as in *kite*

Use this QR code to watch and listen to the **letter I_E** sound cards below

 kite	 bike
 mine	 slide

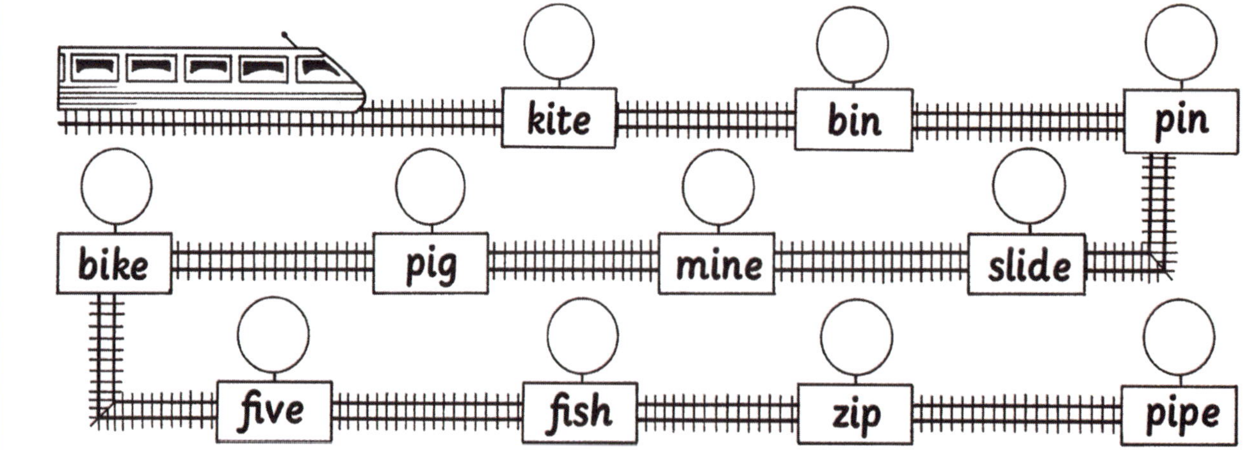

The train will stop for long **i** words. Tick the 6 boxes with the long **i** words.

  ISBN: 9781925726350

Long vowel sound i with split digraph i_e as in *kite*

Say the names of the pictures. Write the word below.
Don't forget the 'e' on the end.

Handwriting

Trace the words then copy them onto the lines below.

  ISBN: 9781925726350

Consonant sound  with the digraph ch as in *chips*

Use this QR code to watch and listen to the **letter CH** sound cards below

 chips	 church
 chick	 beach

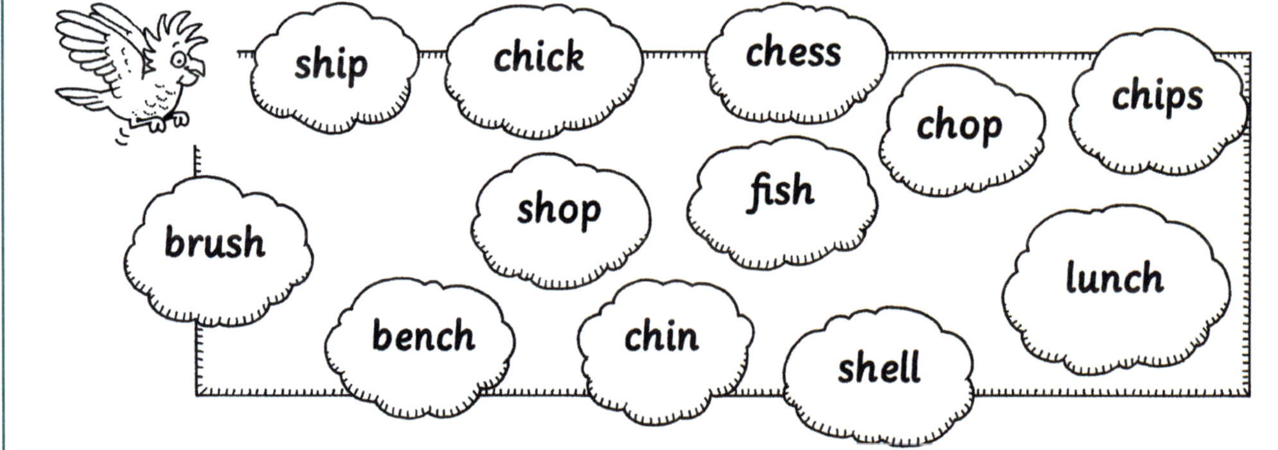

Cocky likes to fly through clouds with the ***ch*** sound.
Colour them for her.

  ISBN: 9781925726350

Consonant sound ch with the digraph ch as in *chips*

Say the names of the pictures. Listen for the 'ch' sound. Write the word below.

Handwriting

Trace the words then copy them onto the lines below.

  ISBN: 9781925726350

⋆ Unit 1 Review ⋆

Consonant sounds 'sh' and 'ch', and long vowel sounds 'a' and 'i' with split digraphs. Read the words. Draw lines to match them to the pictures.

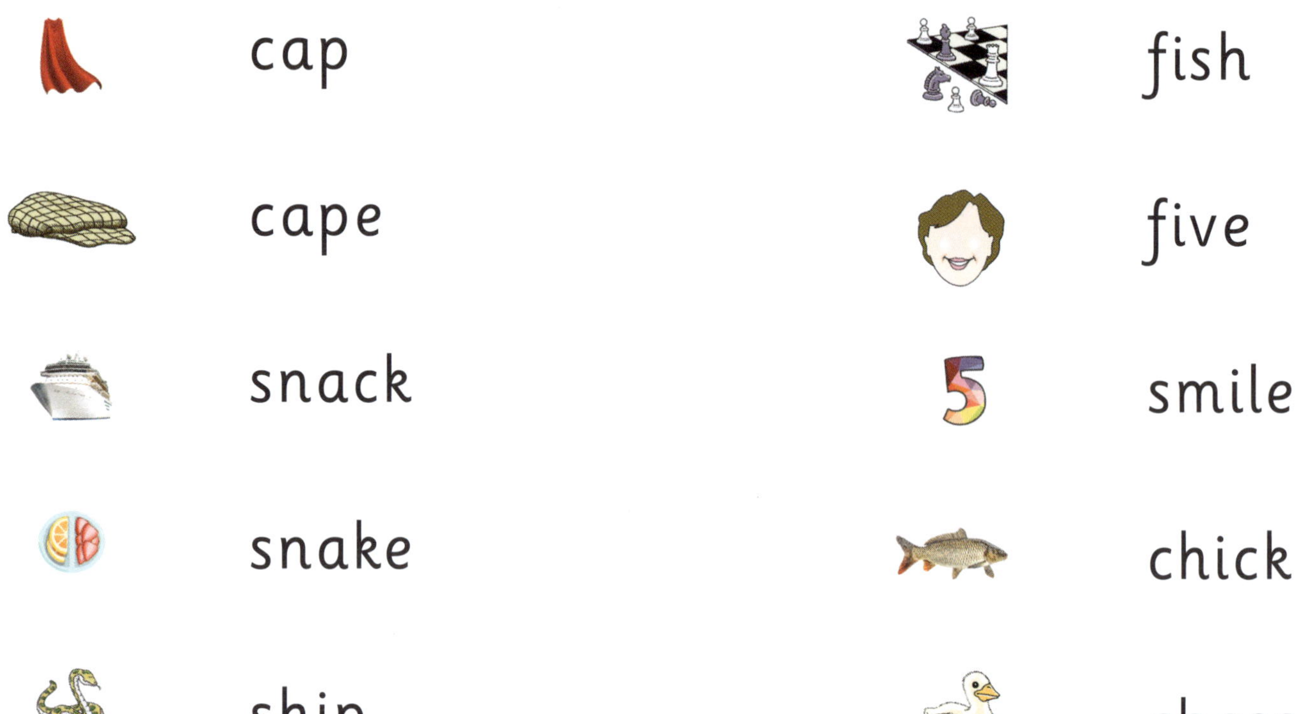

Say the names of the pictures below. Write the letters that are missing from each word.

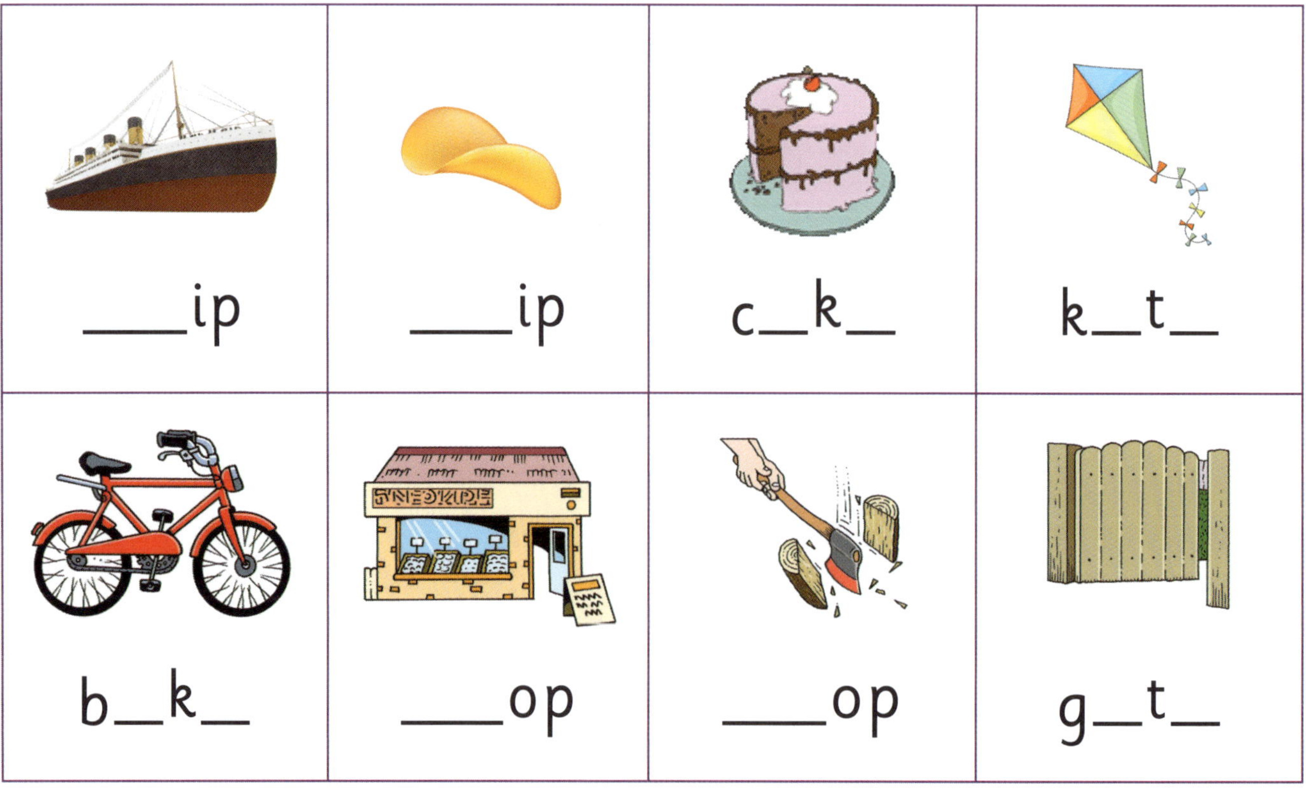

  ISBN: 9781925726350

Long vowel sounds 'a' and 'i' with split digraphs

The *e* on the end makes the vowel in the middle turn from short to long. The *e* on the end of the word helps the *a* say its name, but the *e* says nothing. It is silent. Read these pairs of words.

can cane tap tape

The *e* on the end of the word helps the *i* say its name, but the *e* says nothing. It is silent.

pin pine rip ripe

Read and draw

Write the e on the end of each word. Then draw a picture of the word you made.

cak_	snak_	gat_
kit_	bik_	pip_

Choose the correct word

Look at the pictures. Read the pairs of words. Circle the correct word.

can cane	ship chip	shop chop
bake bike	kit kite	bunch bush

  ISBN: 9781925726350

⋆ Consonant sounds ‘sh’ and ‘ch’ ⋆

Decoding

Now you know these letters and sounds. You can blend them to make and read these words.

Say the sounds	Blend the sounds	Read the word
Point to each letter as you say the sound.	Slide your finger from one sound to the next as you say the sound.	Point to the word as you read it.
r i ch	r‿i‿ch	rich
w i sh	w‿i‿sh	wish
sh o t	sh‿o‿t	shot
ch o p	ch‿o‿p	chop
sh e d	sh‿e‿d	shed
ch i ck	ch‿i‿ck	chick
b e n ch	b‿e‿n‿ch	bench
f i sh	f‿i‿sh	fish
ch a m p	ch‿a‿m‿p	champ
sh u t	sh‿u‿t	shut

Spelling

Say the names of the pictures below. Stretch out the word to hear the sound at the beginning, the sound in the middle and the sound at the end. Write the words on the lines below. Don’t forget the ‘e’ on the end if you need it.

  ISBN: 9781925726350

Handwriting

Now you can read these words, you can write them too.

Trace the words. Then write them on the lines below.

shake prize time

champ chime chase

shine shape shell

  ISBN: 9781925726350

High frequency words – Unit 1

Here are some high frequency words to learn by sight.

your	day	play	his	her
all	their	after	she	came

Comprehension

Read the sentences. Draw a picture to match.

Dad went in the shed. The pup went in the shed after him. The cat ran away from the shed.	I like chops for lunch. Mum likes chops for lunch. Dad likes chops for lunch. We all like chops.

"Can I play with your big red van?" said the little boy. "Yes, if I can play with your little black truck," said the big boy.	The girl ran after her pet dog. The dog ran after a cat. The cat went after a bug. The cat got the bug.

  ISBN: 9781925726350

Comprehension

Look at the pictures. Read the sentences. Write in the missing word.

I have a __ __ __ __ for you. I got it at the shop.

We all like to have __ __ __ __ and __ __ __ __ __ for lunch.

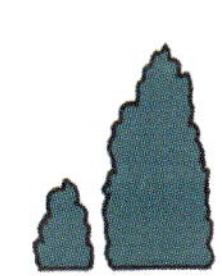

I can ride my __ __ __ __ down the hill.

This sentence is jumbled. Write it correctly on the lines below.

fish had We lunch. and for chips

  ISBN: 9781925726350

Long vowel sound 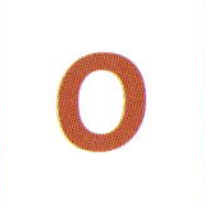 with split digraph o_e as in *home*

Use this QR code to watch and listen to the **letter O_E** sound cards below

 home	 rope
 pole	 stone

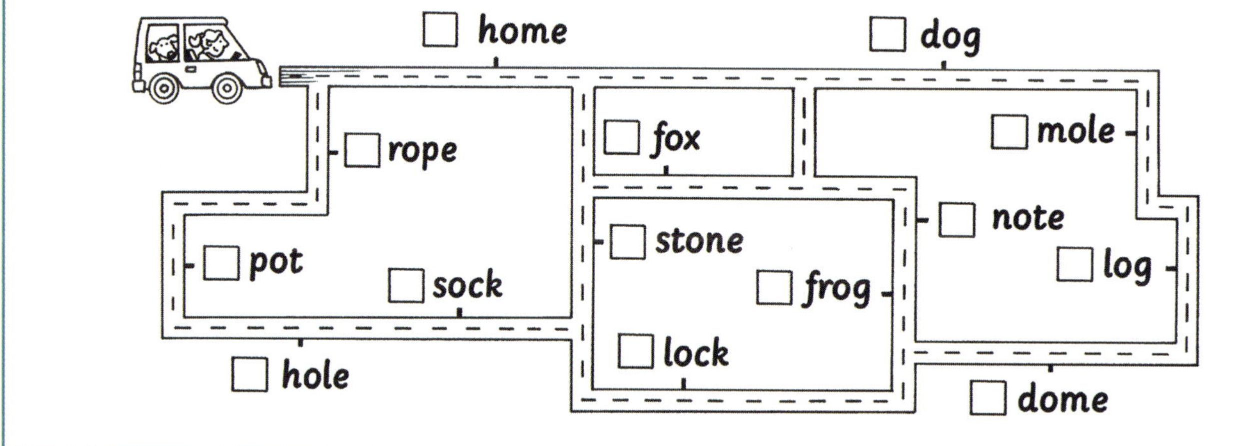

Jenna needs to stop her car at words with a long o. Tick the boxes for her.

  ISBN: 9781925726350

Long vowel sound o with split digraph o_e as in *home*

Say the names of the pictures. Write the word below.
Don't forget the 'e' on the end.

Handwriting

Trace the words then copy them onto the lines below.

  ISBN: 9781925726350

Consonant sound th with the digraph th as in *father (voiced)*

Use this QR code to watch and listen to the **letter TH** sound cards below

 father	 brother
 this	 that

Put a cross next to the words that don't have a **th** sound and tick the others.

 © PASCAL PRESS ISBN: 9781925726350

Consonant sound th with the digraph th as in *father (voiced)*

Say the names of the pictures. Listen for the 'th' sound. Colour the pictures with the 'th' sound as in 'father'.

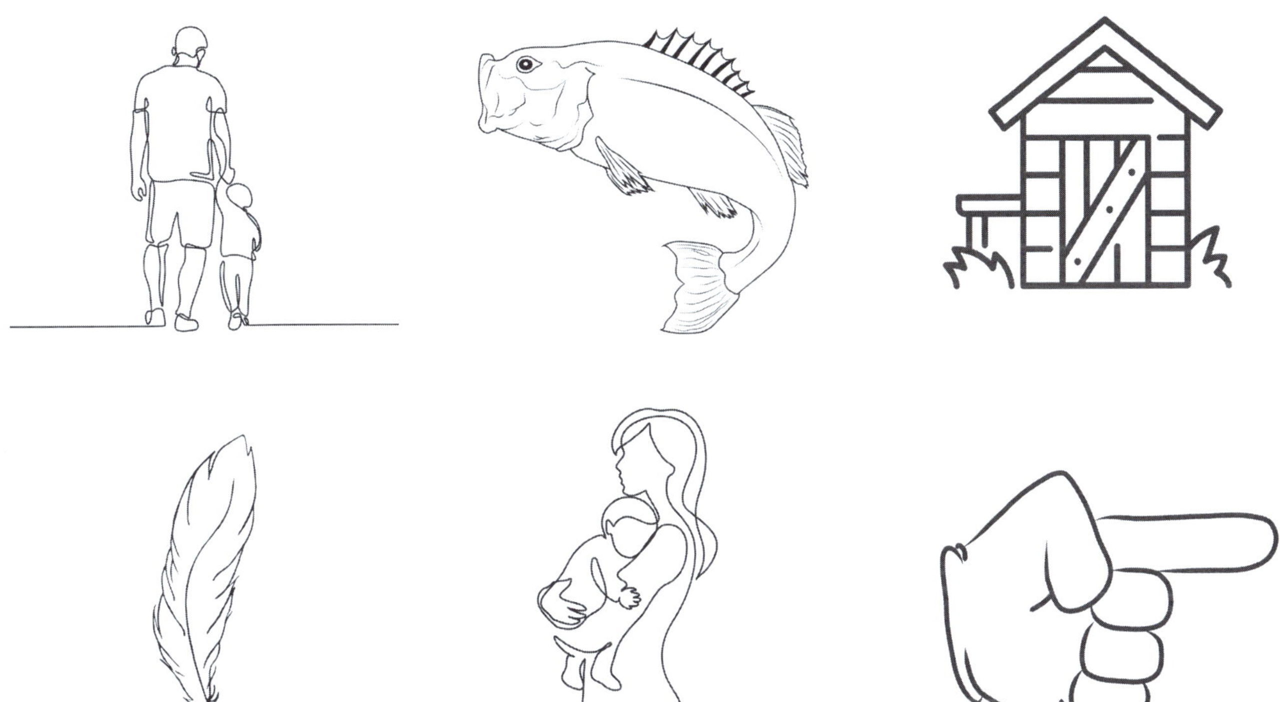

Handwriting

Trace the words then copy them onto the lines below.

  ISBN: 9781925726350

Long vowel sound  u with split digraph u_e as in *mule*

Use this QR code to watch and listen to the **letter U_E** sound cards below

 mule	 huge
 cube	 cute

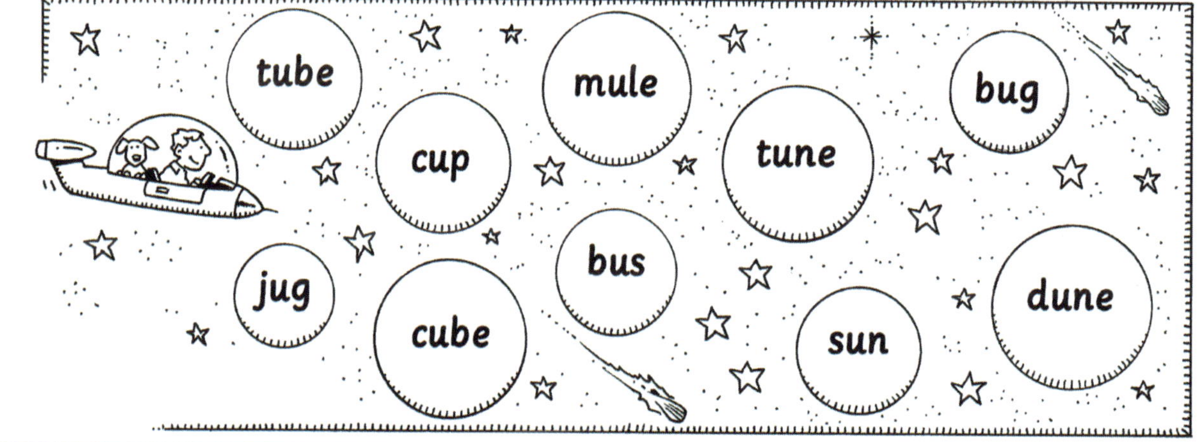

Boris needs to find all the long **u** planets. Colour them so he can find them.

  ISBN: 9781925726350

Long vowel sound u with split digraph u_e as in *mule*

Say the names of the pictures. Write the word below.
Don't forget the 'e' on the end.

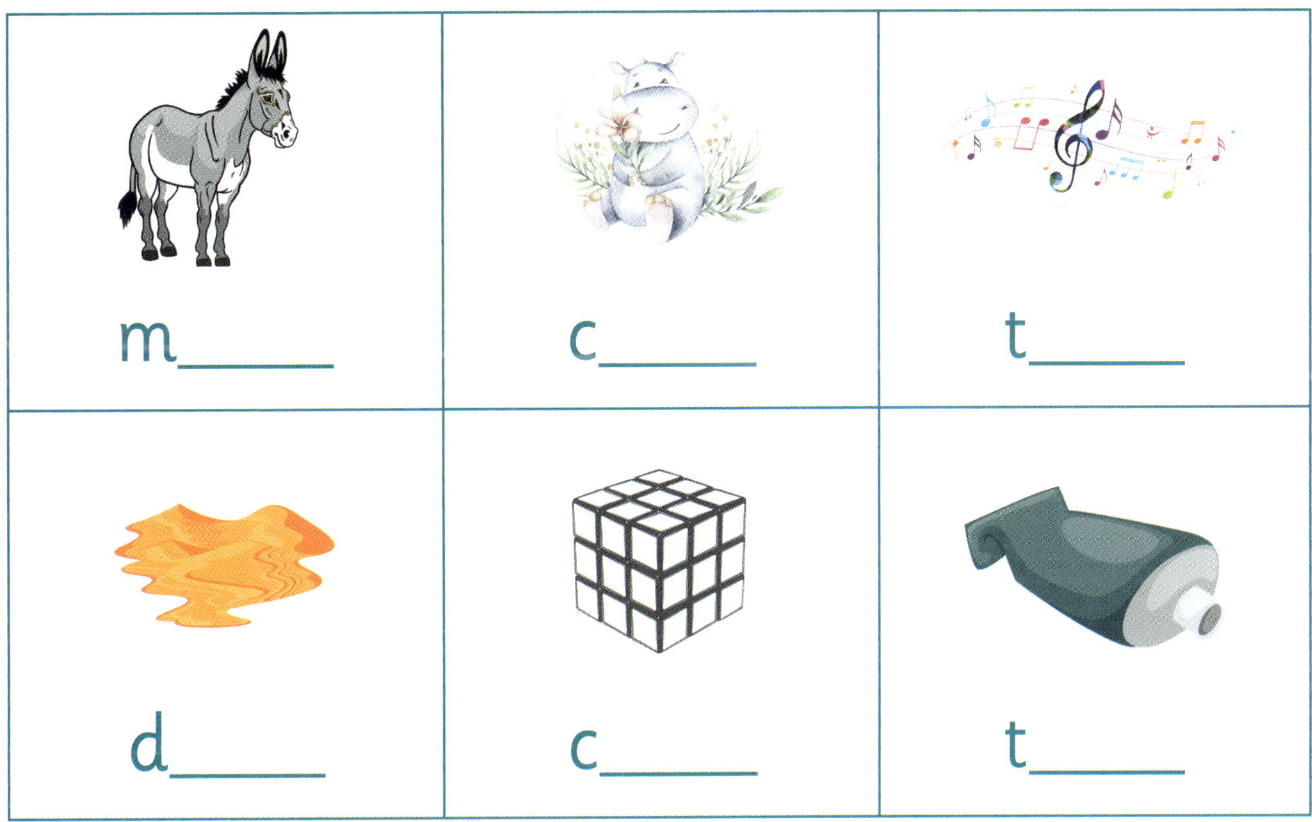

Handwriting

Trace the words then copy them onto the lines below.

  ISBN: 9781925726350

Consonant sound  with the digraph th as in *think (unvoiced)*

Use this QR code to watch and listen to the **letter TH** sound cards below

 think	 throne
 moth	 bath

Colour in all the words that have a **th** sound.

  ISBN: 9781925726350

Consonant sound th with the digraph th as in *think* (unvoiced)

Say the names of the pictures. Listen for the 'th' sound. Write the word below.

Handwriting

Trace the words then copy them onto the lines below.

  ISBN: 9781925726350

⋆ Unit 2 Review ⋆

Consonant sounds 'th' (voiced and unvoiced), and long vowel sounds 'o' and 'u' with split digraphs. Read the words. Draw lines to match them to the pictures.

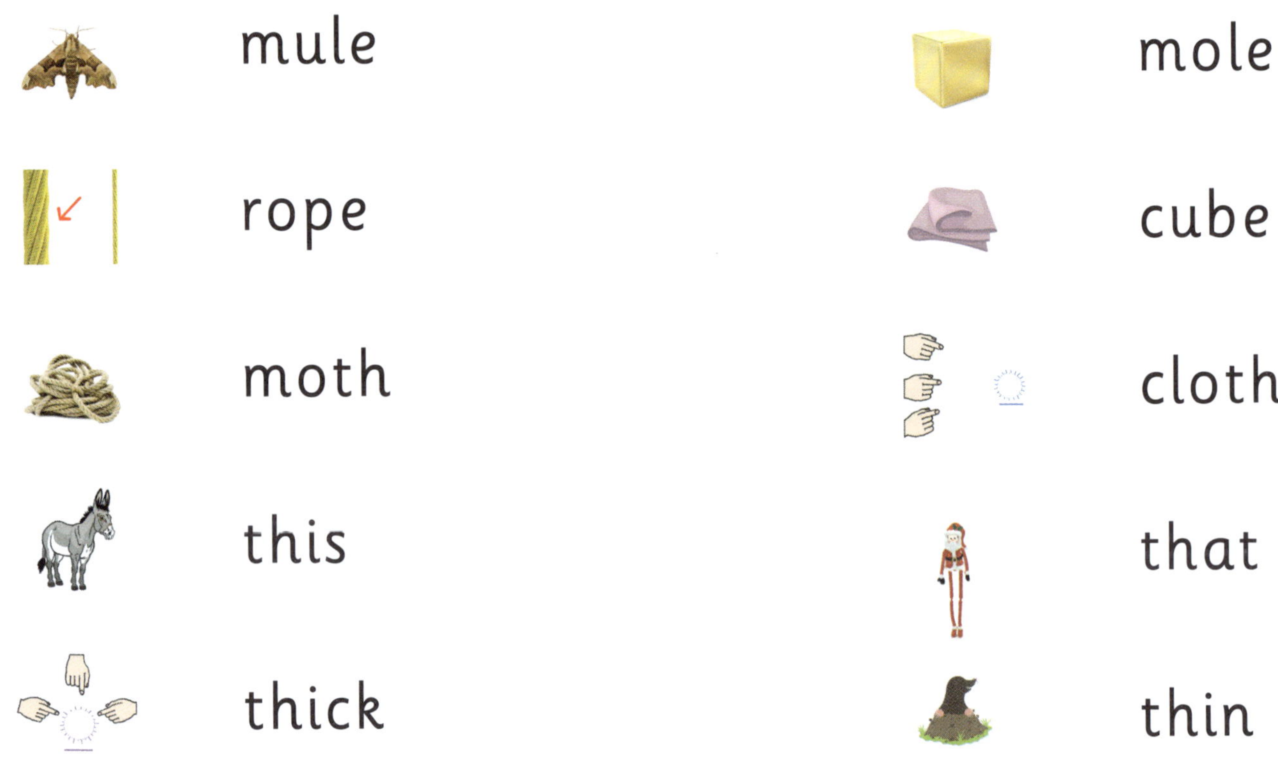

Say the names of the pictures below. Write the letters that are missing from each word.

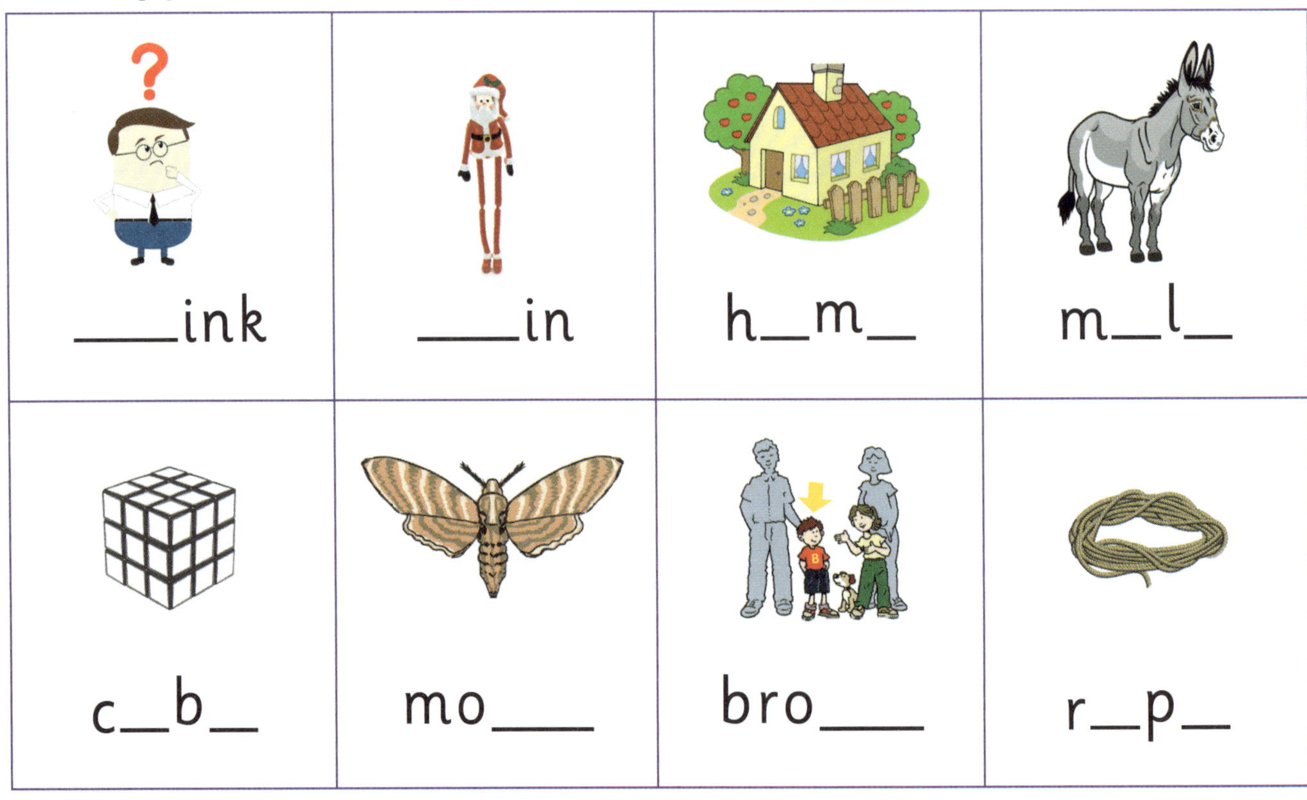

  ISBN: 9781925726350

Long vowel sounds 'o' and 'u' with split digraphs

The *e* on the end makes the vowel in the middle turn from short to long. The *e* on the end of the word helps the *o* say its name, but the *e* says nothing. It is silent. Read these pairs of words.

rob robe mop mope

The *e* on the end of the word helps the *u* say its name, but the *e* says nothing. It is silent. Read these pairs of words.

cut cute cub cube

Read and draw

Write the e on the end of each word. Then draw a picture of the word you made.

mol_	hom_	rop_
mul_	tub_	cub_

Choose the correct word

Look at the pictures. Read the pairs of words. Circle the correct word.

mole mule	cub cube	thick thin
moth broth	moth them	think thank

  ISBN: 9781925726350

★ Consonant sounds 'th' (voiced and unvoiced) ★

(Note: the first five are voiced. The second five are unvoiced.)

Decoding

Now you know these letters and sounds. You can blend them to make and read these words.

Say the sounds	Blend the sounds	Read the word
Point to each letter as you say the sound.	Slide your finger from one sound to the next as you say the sound.	Point to the word as you read it.
th i s	th i s	this
th a t	th a t	that
th e n	th e n	then
th e m	th e m	them
th a n	th a n	than
th i ck	th i ck	thick
th i n	th i n	thin
w i th	w i th	with
th i n k	th i n k	think
m o th	m o th	moth

Spelling

Say the names of the pictures below. Stretch out the word to hear the sound at the beginning, the sound in the middle and the sound at the end. Write the words on the lines below. Don't forget the 'e' on the end if you need it.

  ISBN: 9781925726350

Handwriting

Now you can read these words, you can write them too.

Trace the words. Then write them on the lines below.

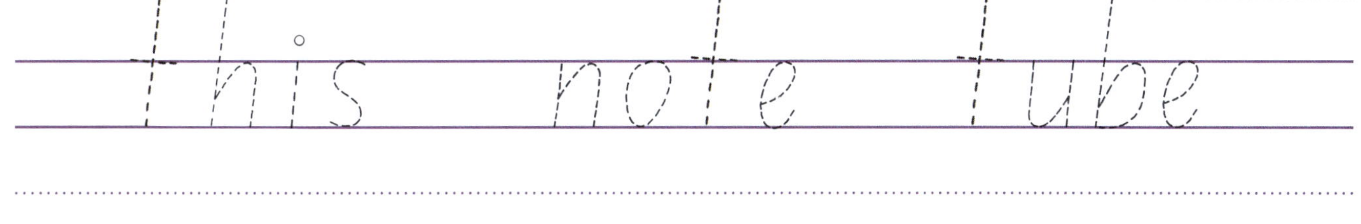

cute hope moth

with think hole

  ISBN: 9781925726350

High frequency words – Unit 2

Here are some high frequency words to learn by sight.

walk	by	be	stay	water
brother	sister	out	please	saw

Comprehension

Read the sentences. Draw a picture to match.

I went with my brother for a walk. We went by the lake. We saw five big ducks and six little ducks. They can swim in the water.	My sister will not stay in the tent. She said that it is too hot. She can not play her game. "Can we go home, please?" she said.

The boy rode his bike. He rode with his sister. They rode out in the lane. They rode away down the lane. Then they rode back home.	I think I will be the champ. I have a rope. I have a pole. I have a net. I will get ten fish in my net. I will win!

  ISBN: 9781925726350

Comprehension

Look at the pictures. Read the sentences. Write in the missing word.

A cute cat in a red cape sat on a

__ __ __ __.

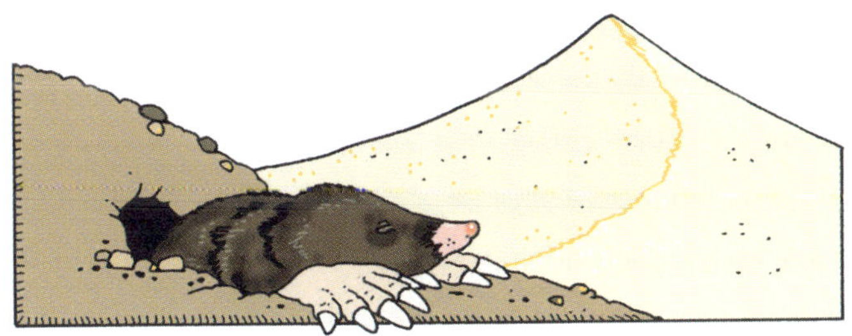

A mole was in a __ __ __ __ at the side of the dune.

The boy rode a

__ __ __ __

down the lane.

This sentence is jumbled. Write it correctly on the lines below.

have and brother I home. a sister a at

  ISBN: 9781925726350

Long vowel sound  as in *rain* and *play*

You already know how to read and spell words with the long vowel sound 'a' with a split digraph as in 'cake'. Now you will learn how to read and spell other ways of writing the long vowel sound 'a'.

Use this QR code to watch and listen to the **letter AI** sound cards below

rain

play

eight

snake

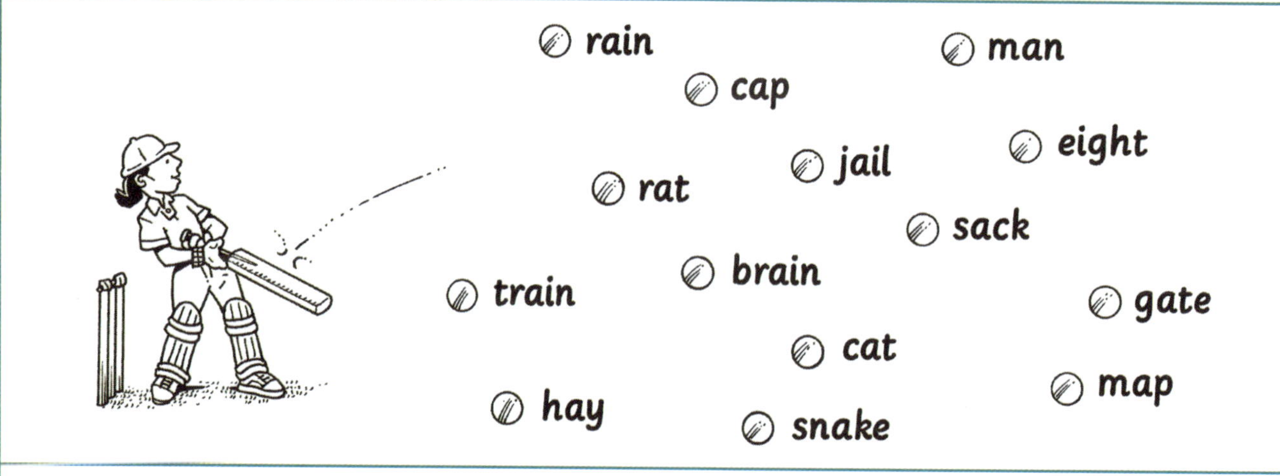

Colour the fast bowler's balls red - they are using a short **a**.
Colour the spin bowler's balls yellow, they use a long **a**.

Long vowel sound *a* as in *train* and *play*

Say the names of the pictures. Listen for the long 'a' sound. Spell the long 'a' sound 'ai'.

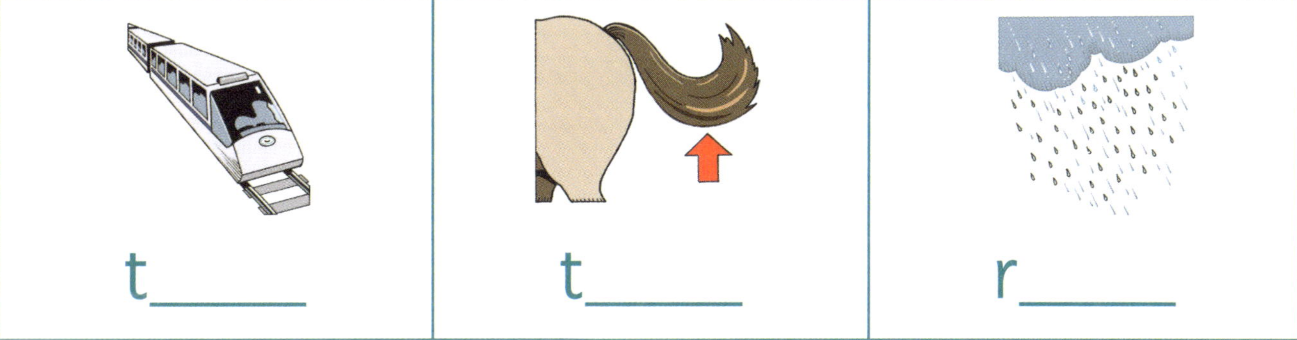

Say the names of the pictures. Listen for the long 'a' sound. Spell the long 'a' sound 'ay'.

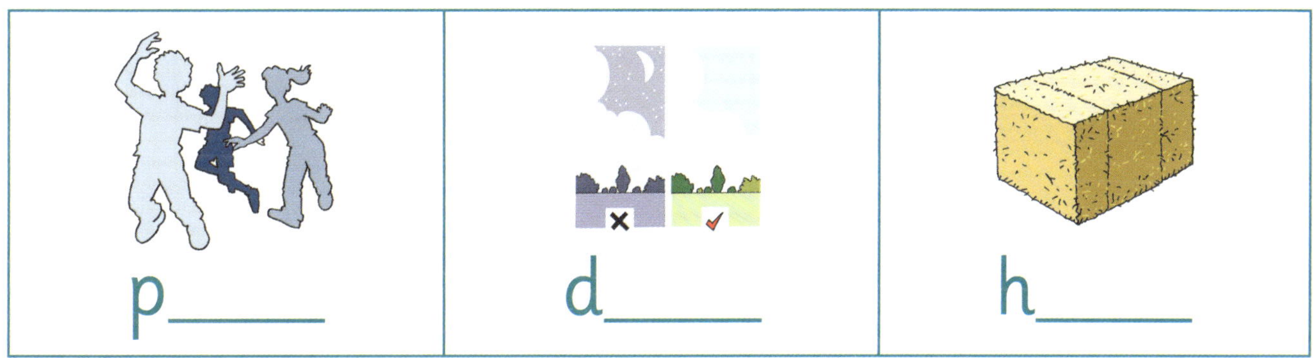

Handwriting

Trace the words then copy them onto the lines below.

  ISBN: 9781925726350

Consonant sound  with the digraph ph as in *phone*

ph

You already know about the consonant sound 'f'. Now you will learn that the letters 'ph' together also spell the consonant sound 'f' like in 'phone'.

Use this QR code to watch and listen to the **letter PH** sound cards below

 phone	 photo
 elephant	 dolphin

Can you find and colour 5 words with a **ph** in them?

  ISBN: 9781925726350

Consonant sound *f* with the digraph *ph* as in *phone*

Say the names of the pictures. Listen for the 'f' sound.
Write 'ph' in the space to complete the word.

Handwriting

Trace the words then copy them onto the lines below.

 © PASCAL PRESS ISBN: 9781925726350

Long vowel sound e as in *bee* and *beach*

Use this QR code to watch and listen to the **letter EE** sound cards below

 bee	 beach
 emu	 me

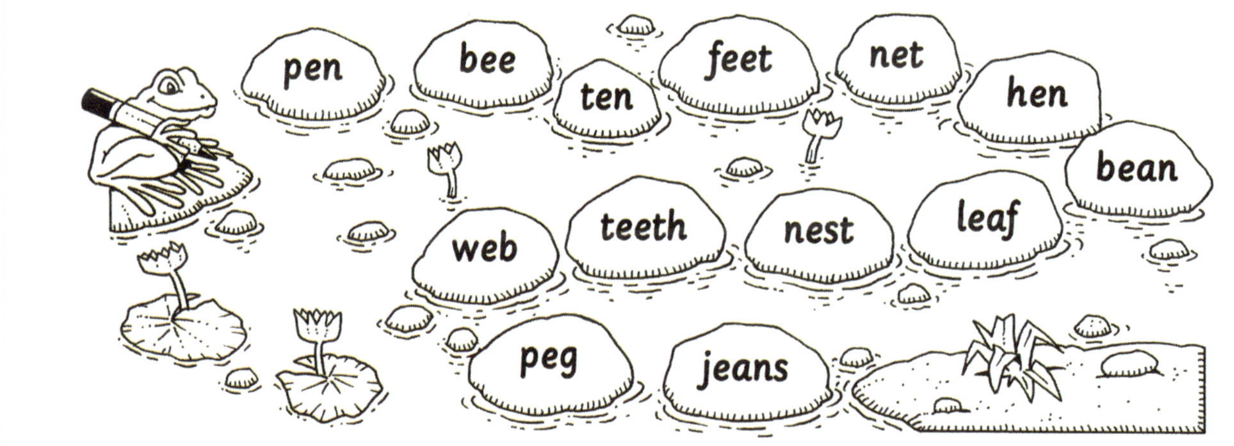

Ferdie likes to colour the long **e** stepping stones green.
Can you help him?

  ISBN: 9781925726350

Long vowel sound *e* as in *bee* and *beach*

Say the names of the pictures. Listen for the long 'e' sound.
Spell the long 'e' sound 'ee'.

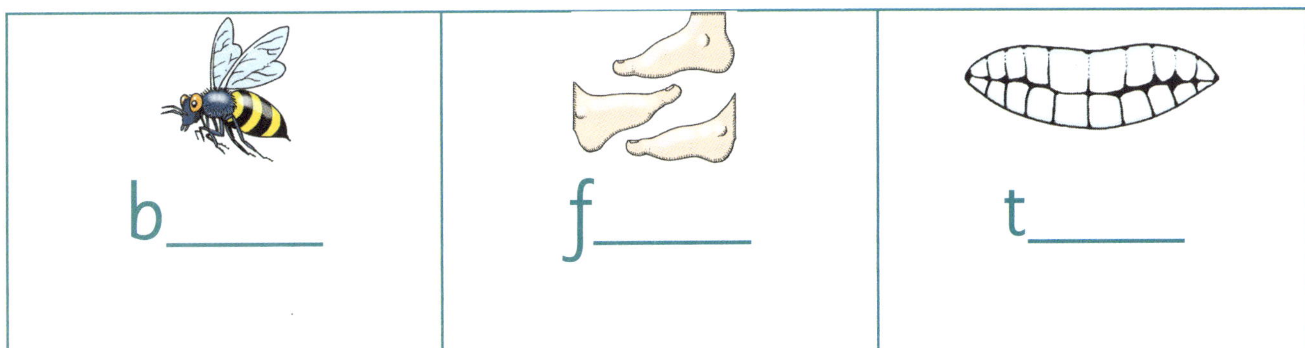

Say the names of the pictures. Listen for the long 'e' sound.
Spell the long 'e' sound 'ea'.

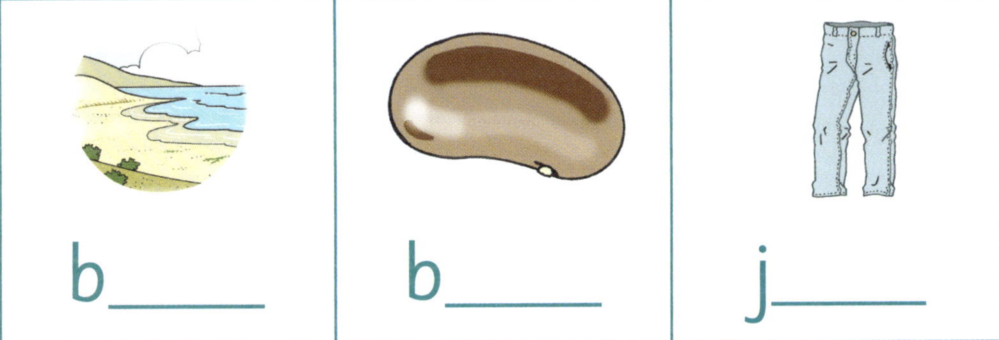

Did you know?

The letter 'y' on the end of a word sometimes spells the long consonant 'e' sound, as in 'happy' and 'baby'.

Handwriting

Trace the words then copy them onto the lines below.

  ISBN: 9781925726350

Consonant sound ng with the digraph ng as in *ring*

Use this QR code to watch and listen to the **letter NG** sound cards below

ng

 ring	 sing
 king	 wing

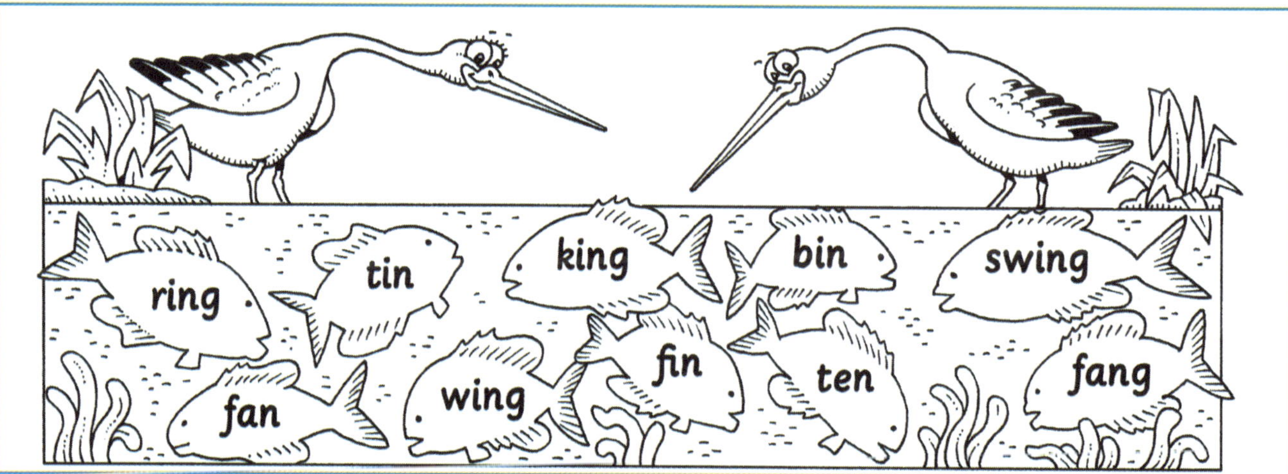

Help Iris and Ivan catch their favourite **ng** word fishes by colouring their fins red.

  ISBN: 9781925726350

Consonant sound *ng* with the digraph *ng* as in *ring*

Say the names of the pictures. Listen for the 'ng' sound. Write the word below.

Handwriting

Trace the words then copy them onto the lines below.

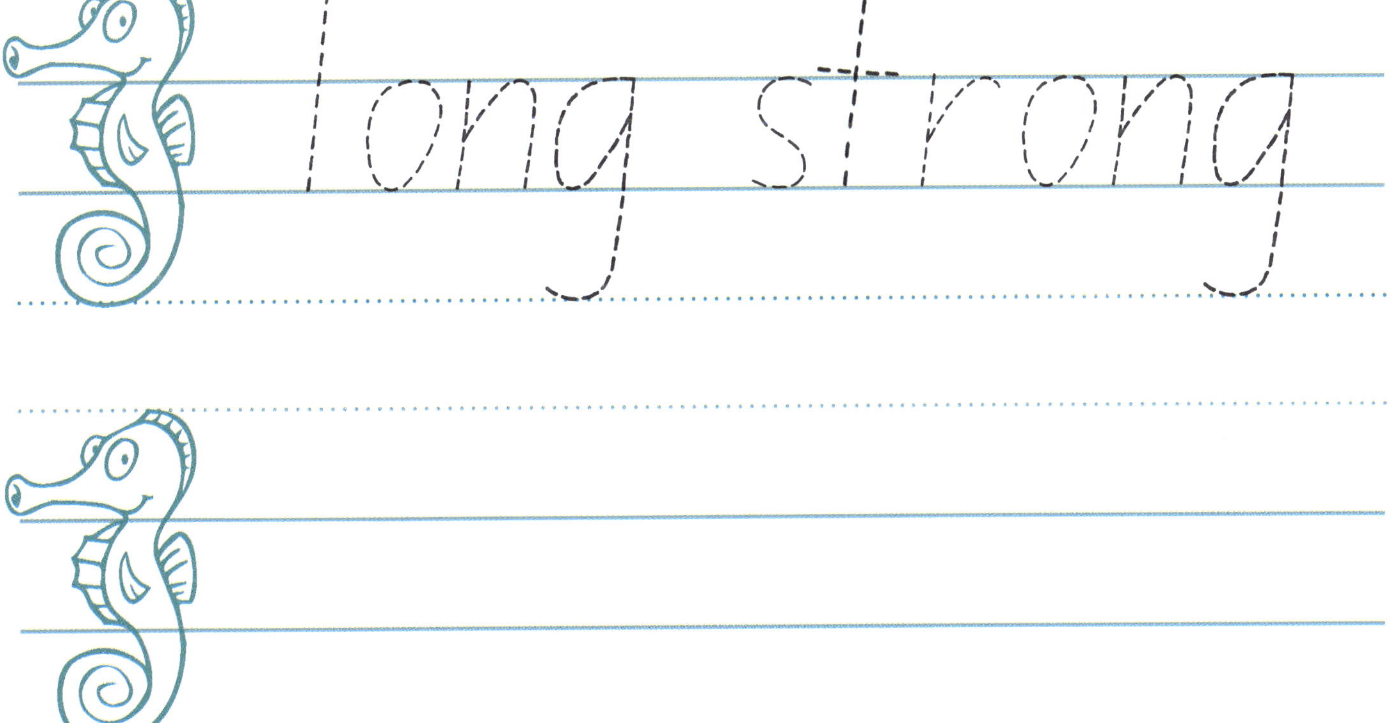

  ISBN: 9781925726350

★ Unit 3 Review ★

Consonant sounds 'ph' and 'ng', and long vowel sounds 'a' and 'e'.
Read the words. Draw lines to match them to the pictures.

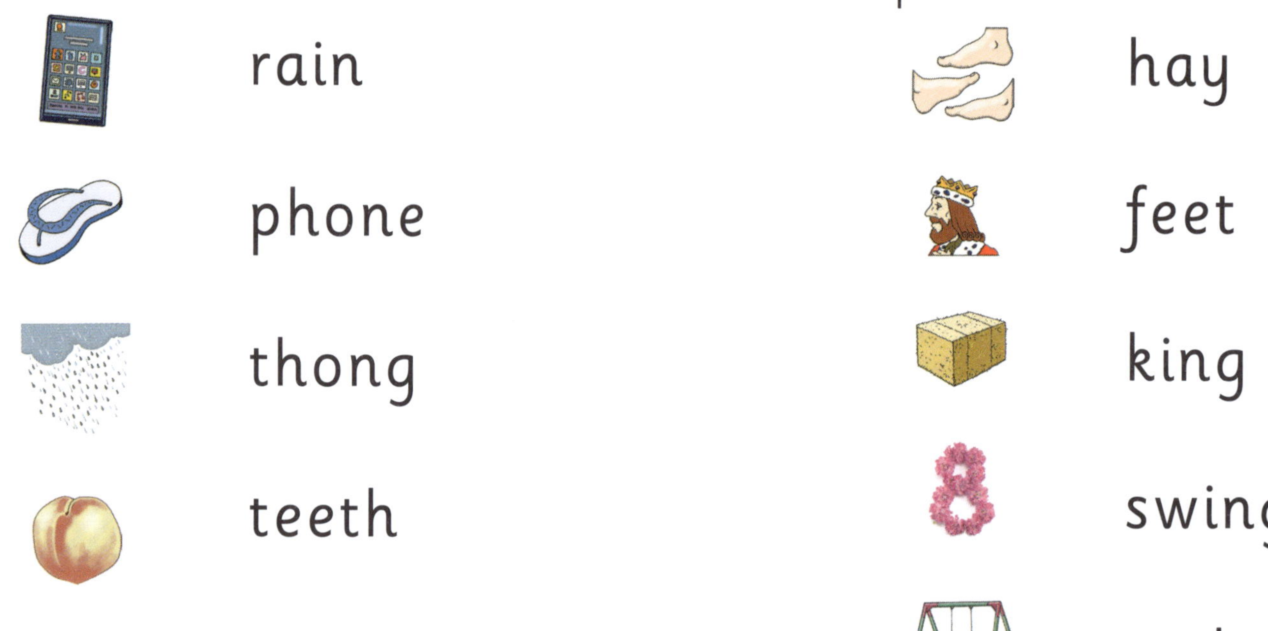

Spelling

Say the names of the pictures below. Stretch out the word to hear the sound at the beginning, the sound in the middle and the sound at the end. Write the words on the lines below. Don't forget the 'e' on the end if you need it.

ph___	sh___	sn___	h___
b___	___ng	___ng	b___

  ISBN: 9781925726350

Long vowel sound *a*

There are different ways to spell the long *a* sound as in *cake*.
Decode to read these words.

a_e

cake

cake
snake
shade
game
mate

ai

rain

snail
pail
plain
paid
mail

ay

hay

tray
say
play
may
stay

eigh

eight

eight
freight
weight
neigh
sleigh

Read and draw

Finish the words with a_e, ai or ay. Then draw a picture of the word you made.

sn__k__	d___	tr___n
h___	b__k___	r___n

Long vowel sound *e*

There are different ways to spell the long *e* sound as in *sheep*.
Decode to read these words.

ee

sheep

sheep
seed
green
teeth
bee

ea

bean

bead
peach
teach
eat
sea

e

me

me
he
she
be

Read and draw

Finish the words with ee, ea or e. Then draw a picture of the word you made.

tr___	m___	b___ch
s___l	gr___n	l___f

  ISBN: 9781925726350

⋆ Consonant sound ‘ng’ ⋆

Decoding

Now you know these letters and sounds. You can blend them to make and read these words.

Say the sounds	Blend the sounds	Read the word
Point to each letter as you say the sound.	Slide your finger from one sound to the next as you say the sound.	Point to the word as you read it.
r i ng	r‿i‿ng	ring
w i ng	w‿i‿ng	wing
l o ng	l‿o‿ng	long
s o ng	s‿o‿ng	song
h a ng	h‿a‿ng	hang
s w i ng	s‿w‿i‿ng	swing
b r i ng	b‿r‿i‿ng	bring
d i ng	d‿i‿ng	ding
c l a ng	c‿l‿a‿ng	clang
s l i ng	s‿l‿i‿ng	sling

Spelling

Say the names of the pictures below. Stretch out the word to hear the sound at the beginning, the sound in the middle and the sound at the end. Write the words on the lines below.

  ISBN: 9781925726350

Handwriting

Now you can read these words, you can write them too.
Trace the words. Then write them on the lines below.

hail play eight

feet beach sea

phone king song

  ISBN: 9781925726350

High frequency words – Unit 3

Here are some high frequency words to learn by sight.

as	put

Comprehension

Read the sentences. Draw a picture to match.

I got a ring and a neck chain as a prize. They have a red stone. I gave them to my sister. She put them on.	We went to the beach. It was a fun day. We sang a song on the way. We like to play on the sand and in the water.

Mum gave me her phone. "You can play a game," she said. I like to play games on Mum's phone.	A snail was on a leaf. The snail will eat the leaf. Dad will not like the snail to eat the leaf. I put it in a pail.

  ISBN: 9781925726350

Comprehension

Look at the pictures. Read the sentences. Write in the missing word.

The boy sang a song for the __ __ __ __.

The girl will teach her brother to play a game on her __ __ __ __ __.

The strong man can lift a big __ __ __ __.

This sentence is jumbled. Write it correctly on the lines below.

hang a Dad play. us will swing for to

  ISBN: 9781925726350

Long vowel sound  as in *pie*, *fly*, and *high*

You already know how to read and spell words with the long vowel sound 'i' with a split digraph as in 'bike'. Now you will learn how to read and spell other ways of writing the long vowel sound 'i'.

Use this QR code to watch and listen to the **letter IE** sound cards below

Find and colour all the flags with long **i** words.

  ISBN: 9781925726350

Long vowel sound *i* as in *pie*, *fly* and *high*

Say the names of the pictures. Listen for the long 'i' sound.
Spell the long 'i' sound 'ie' or 'y'.

Say the names of the pictures. Listen for the long 'i' sound.
Spell the long 'i' sound 'igh'.

Handwriting

Trace the words then copy them onto the lines below.

  ISBN: 9781925726350

Consonant sound  with the digraph wh as in *whale*

Use this QR code to watch and listen to the **letter WH** sound cards below

 whale	 wheat
 whip	 wheel

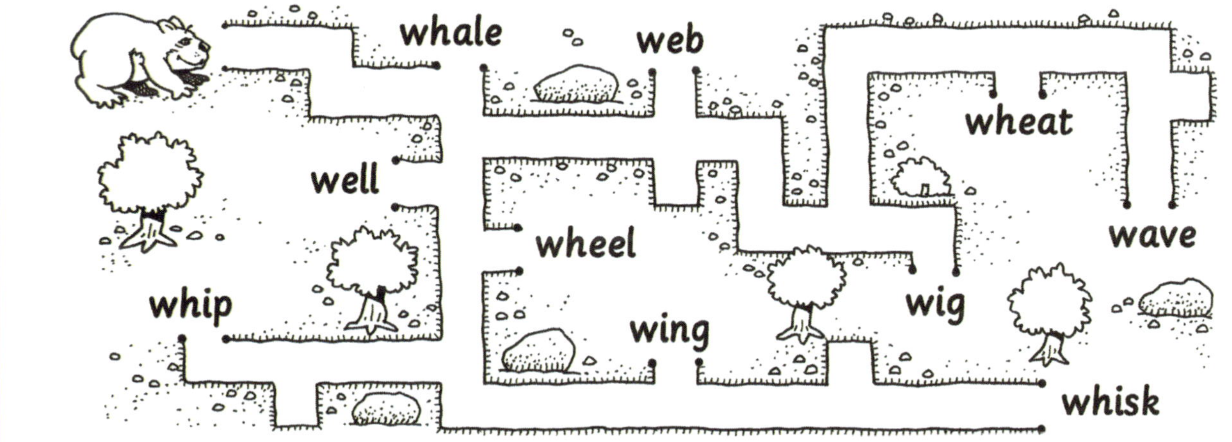

Wombat likes to walk among the **wh** words. Show him where to visit.

  ISBN: 9781925726350

Consonant sound wh with the digraph wh as in *whale*

Say the names of the pictures. Listen for the 'wh' sound.
Write the word below.

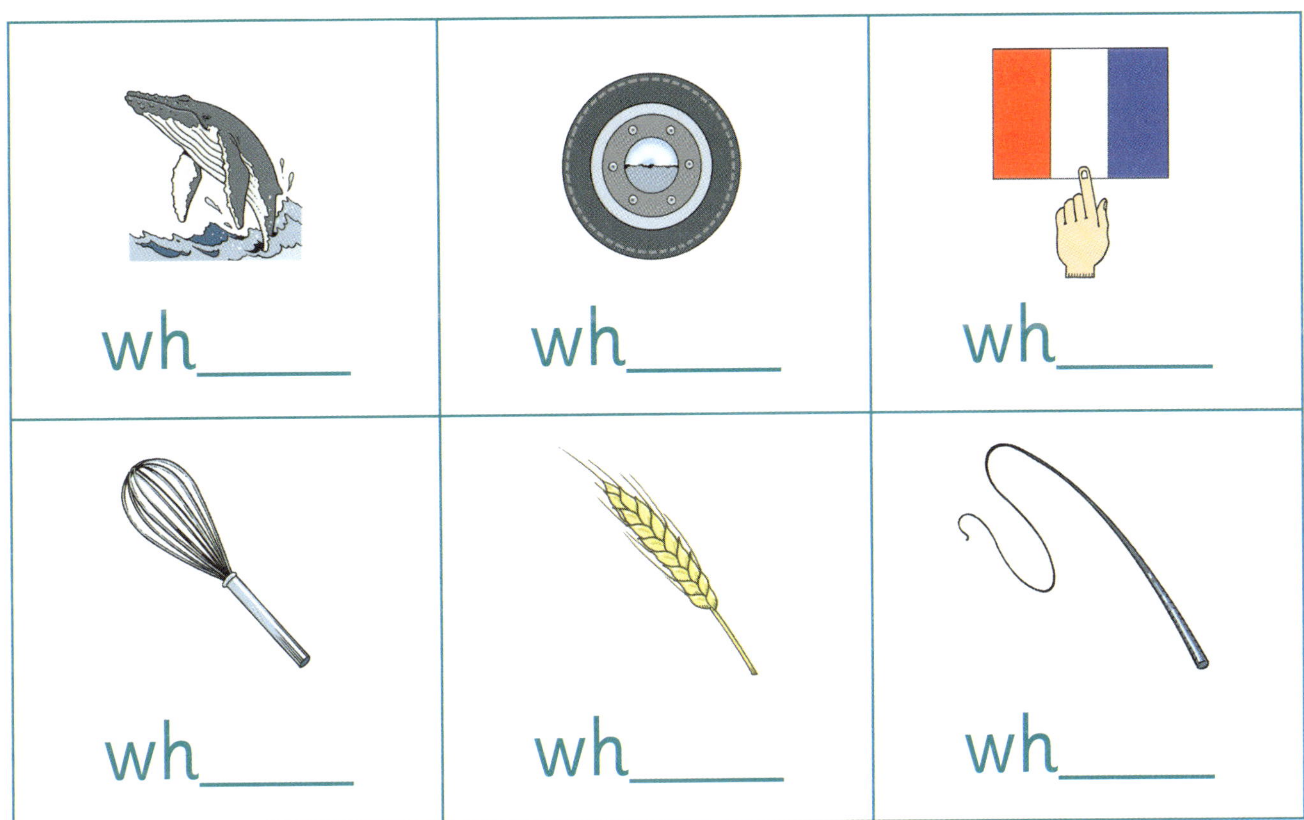

Handwriting

Trace the words then copy them onto the lines below.

  ISBN: 9781925726350

Long vowel sound  as in *boat* and *bow*

You already know how to read and spell words with the long vowel sound 'o' with a split digraph as in 'note'. Now you will learn how to read and spell other ways of writing the long vowel sound 'o'.

Use this QR code to watch and listen to the **letter OA** sound cards below

Mario has to clean all the windows with a long **o** word. How many are there?

  ISBN: 9781925726350

Long vowel sound *o* as in *boat* and *bow*

Say the names of the pictures. Listen for the long 'o' sound.
Spell the long 'o' sound 'oa'.

Say the names of the pictures. Listen for the long 'o' sound.
Spell the long 'o' sound 'oe'.

Handwriting

Trace the words then copy them onto the lines below.

  ISBN: 9781925726350

Consonant sound  as in the *cat*, *kite* and *kick*

You already know that the letters 'c' and 'k' can be used to spell the same sound. Now you will learn that the letter 'c' is often used to spell words when the vowels 'a' 'o' or 'u' come next. The letter 'k' is often used to spell words when the vowels 'i' or 'e' come next. The two letters together spell the sound 'k' in the middle or at the end of a word.

Use this QR code to watch and listen to the **letter CK** sound cards below

Cindy is making a brick wall with **c** and **k** words.
How many end with **ck**?

  ISBN: 9781925726350

Consonant sound *k* as in *cat*, *kite* and *kick*

Say the names of the pictures. Listen for the 'k' sound.
Write the word below.

c_____	k_____	_____ck
k_____	c_____	_____ck

Handwriting

Trace the words then copy them onto the lines below.

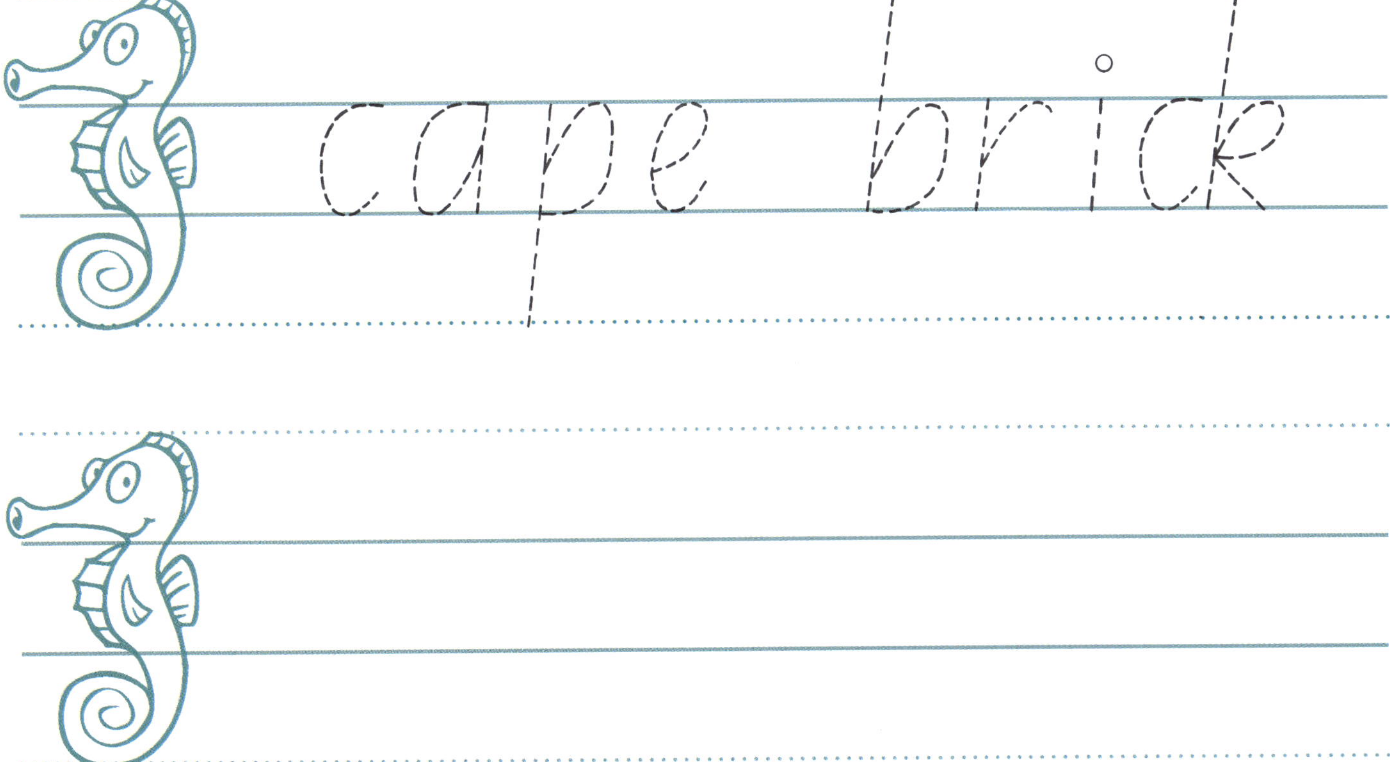

  ISBN: 9781925726350

★ Unit 4 Review ★

Consonant sounds 'wh' and 'k', and long vowel sound 'i' as in pie, fly and high, and long vowel sound 'o' as in boat and bow.

Read the words. Draw lines to match them to the pictures.

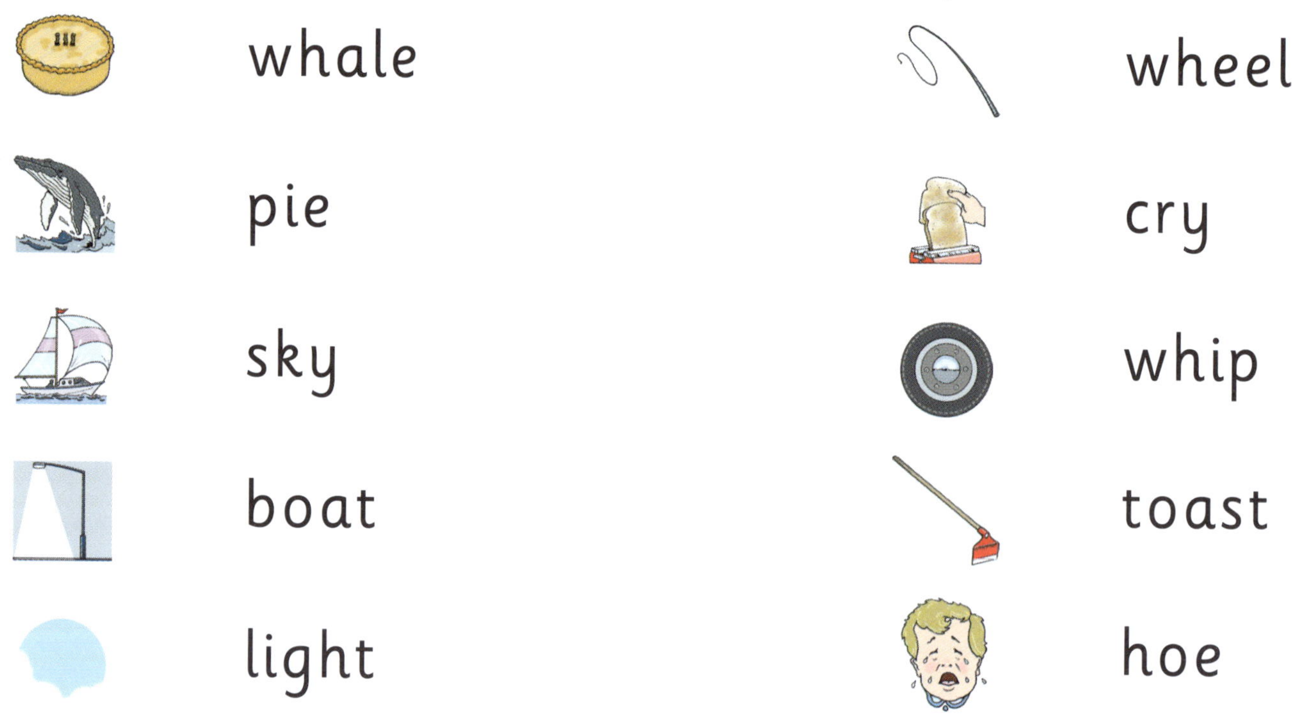

Spelling

Say the names of the pictures below. Write the letters that are missing from each word.

  ISBN: 9781925726350

Long vowel sounds *i*

There are different ways to spell the long *i* sound as in *bike*.
Decode to read these words.

i_e

bike

bike
wipe
fine
time
life

ie

pie

pie
tie
die
lie

y

fly

sky
try
fly
my
spy

igh

light

light
sigh
high
night
fright

Read and draw

Finish the words with i_e, ie, igh or y.
Then draw a picture of the word you made.

Did you know?
Guy and buy also have the long 'i' sound

t___	n___t	fl___
sp___	b__k___	p___

Long vowel sounds *o*

There are different ways to spell the long *o* sound as in *home*.
Decode to read these words.

o_e

home

home
robe
slope
note
bone

oa

boat

boat
float
road
coach
loaf

oe

toe

toe
hoe
doe
foe
floe

ow

bow

bow
slow
tow
show
flow

Read and draw

Finish the words with o_e, oa, oe or ow. Then draw a picture of the word you made.

h___	b___t	s___p
b___	h__m___	l___f

  ISBN: 9781925726350

★ Consonant sound 'wh' ★

Decoding

Now you know these letters and sounds.
You can blend them to make and read these words.

In these **wh** words, the **wh** makes the **h** sound.
who
whose
whom
whole

Say the sounds Point to each letter as you say the sound.	Blend the sounds Slide your finger from one sound to the next as you say the sound.	Read the word Point to the word as you read it.
wh i ch	wh i ch	which
wh i p	wh i p	whip
wh e n	wh e n	when
wh ee l	wh ee l	wheel
wh i s k	wh i s k	whisk
wh ea t	wh ea t	wheat
wh y	wh y	why
wh i t e	wh i t	white
wh a l e	wh a l	whale
wh i l e	wh i l	while

Spelling

Say the names of the pictures below. Stretch out the word to hear the sound at the beginning, the sound in the middle and the sound at the end.

  ISBN: 9781925726350

Handwriting

Now you can read these words, you can write them too.

Trace the words. Then write them on the lines below.

high white wheel

sky float whack

shy when cloak

  ISBN: 9781925726350

High frequency words – Unit 4

Here are some high frequency words to learn by sight.

who	whole	what	guy	buy

Comprehension

Read the sentences. Draw a picture to match.

The boy had a pie for lunch. The girl had fish and chips. They ate the whole lot. They left their plates clean.	The big guy rode his bike to the shop. He went to buy a boat. On the way, his wheel broke. He did not buy a boat. He had to buy a wheel.

The spy has a big black coat. The spy has a big black hat. The spy hides in the black night. He can not be seen.	The boat can float in the sea. It can go high on a wave. The boat has a white sail. When the winds blow, the boat will go.

  ISBN: 9781925726350

Comprehension

Look at the pictures. Read the sentences. Write in the missing word.

A __ __ __ __ __ can fly high in the sky.

A goat in a coat can float in a __ __ __ __.

A big white __ __ __ __ __ can swim in the sea.

This sentence is jumbled. Write it correctly on the lines below.

like my eat jam. I to with toast

  ISBN: 9781925726350

Long vowel sound  oo with split digraph u_e as in *flute*

You already know how to read and spell words with the long vowel sound 'u' with a split digraph as in 'mule'. Now you will learn how to read and spell words that use the same split digraph but have the sound 'oo' as 'flute'.

Use this QR code to watch and listen to the **letter U_E** sound cards below

 flute	 prune
 brute	 June

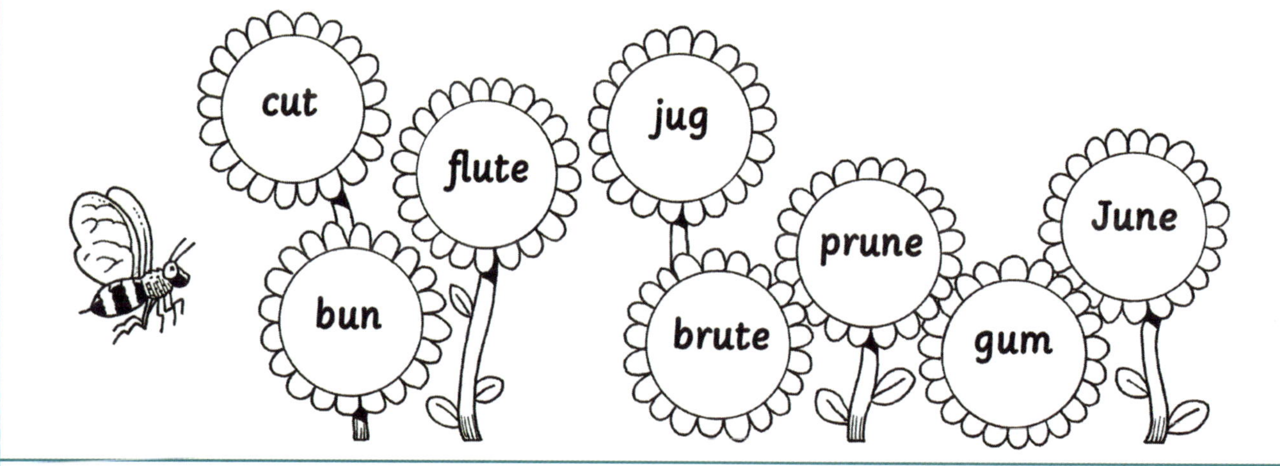

Bizzy bee is visiting her favourite long **u** words (as in flute). How many can you find and colour for her?

  ISBN: 9781925726350

Long vowel sound oo with split digraph u_e as in *flute*

Say the names of the pictures. Write the word below.
Don't forget the 'e' on the end.
These words have the 'oo' sound as in flute.

These words have the 'u' sound as in tube.

Handwriting

Trace the words then copy them onto the lines below.

  ISBN: 9781925726350

Consonant sound soft c as in *cent*

You already know that the letter 'c' is used to spell words when the vowels 'a' 'o' or 'u' come next. That is called the 'hard c' sound. When the letter 'c' is followed by the vowels 'e' or 'i', it makes the sound 's' like in 'snake' and is called a 'soft c' sound. Now you will learn to read and spell words with the soft c sound.

Use this QR code to watch and listen to the **letter C** sound cards below

 cent	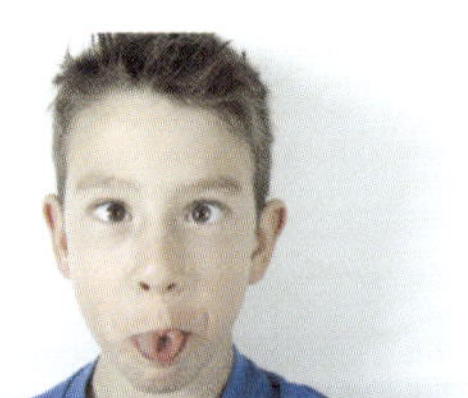 face
 ice	 city

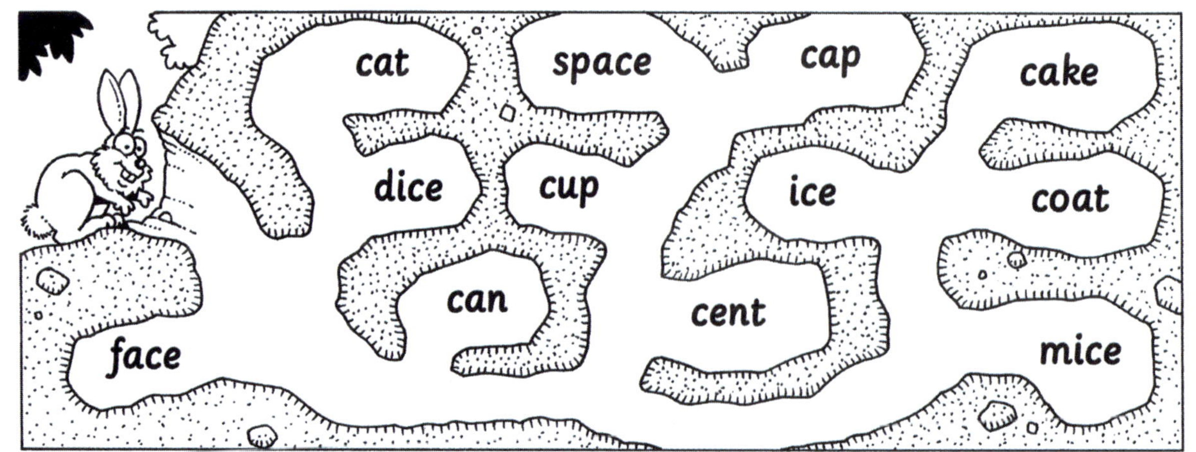

Basil bunny has lots of soft **c** words in his burrow. Find and cirlce them in blue.

  ISBN: 9781925726350

Consonant sound s with the soft c as in *cent*

Say the names of the pictures. Listen for the 'soft c' sound.
Write the word below.

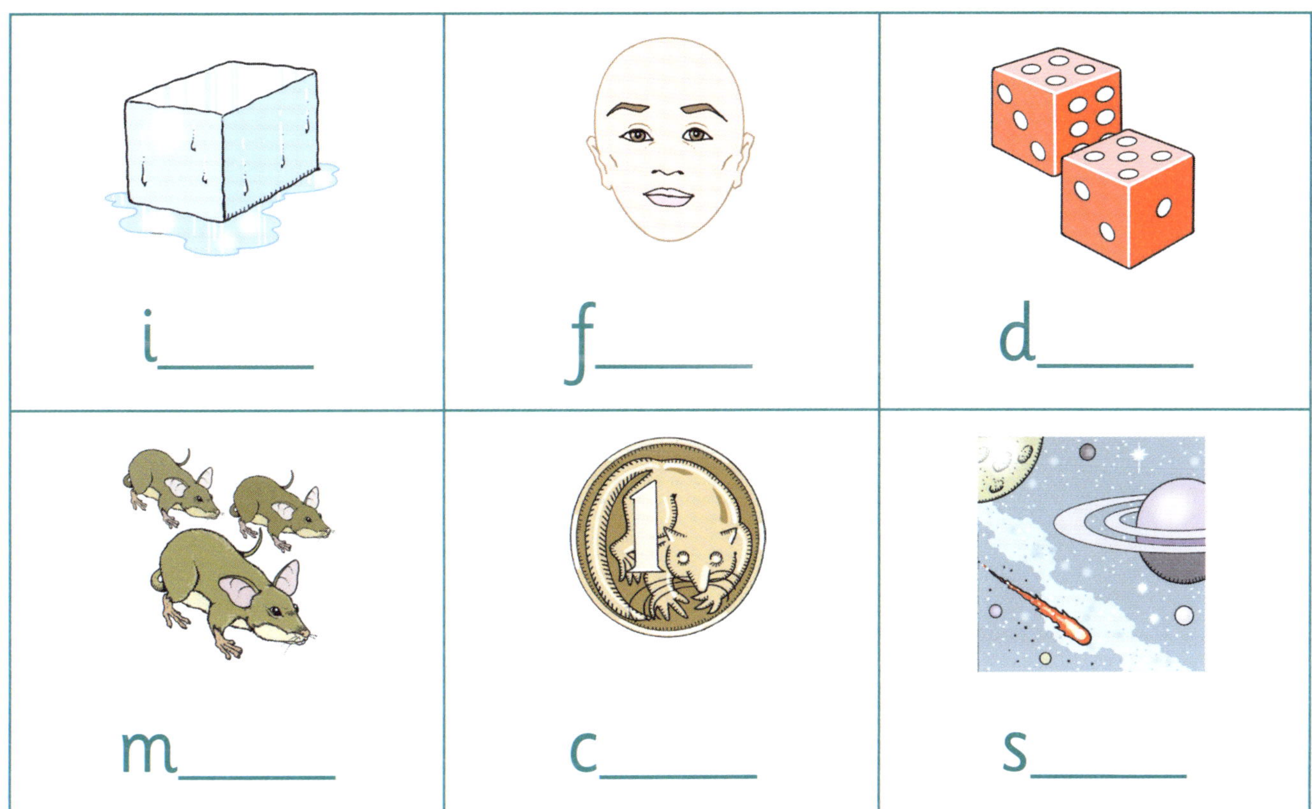

Handwriting

Trace the words then copy them onto the lines below.

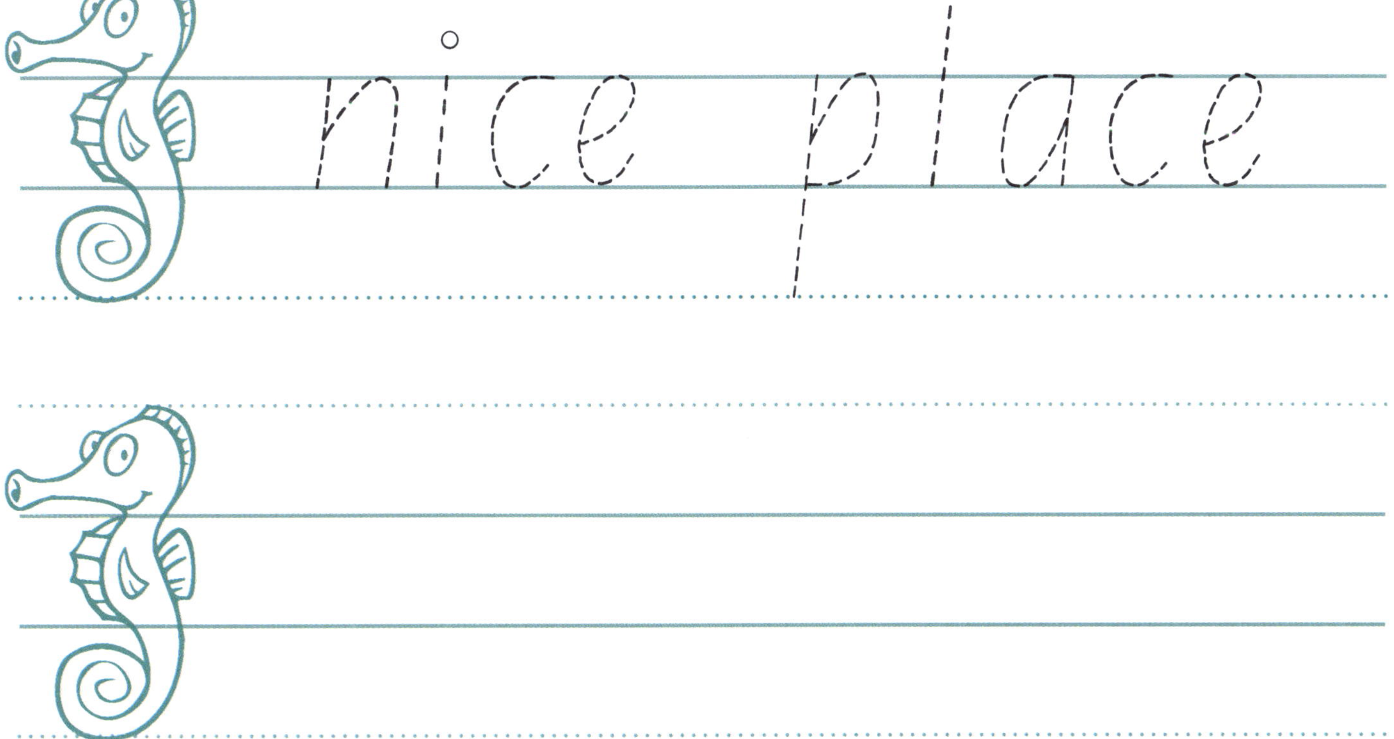

  ISBN: 9781925726350

Long vowel sound oo as in *moon* and *screw*

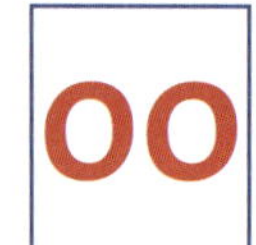

You already know how to spell the long vowel sound 'oo' with the split digraph u_e as in flute. Now you will learn other ways of spelling the long vowel sound 'oo'.

Use this QR code to watch and listen to the **letter OO** sound cards below

moon

blue

stew

fruit

Mandy Moonwalker wants to find out how many **oo** moon words are nearby. Help count them for her.

  ISBN: 9781925726350

Long vowel sound oo as in *moon* and *screw*

Say the names of the pictures. Write the word below.
These words are spelled with 'oo'.

These words are spelled with 'ew'.

Handwriting

Trace the words then copy them onto the lines below.

  ISBN: 9781925726350

Consonant sound j with the soft g as in *gem*

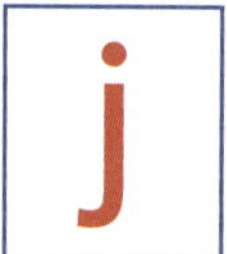

You already know that the letter 'g' is used to spell words such as goat, game and gun. That is called the 'hard g' sound. When the letter 'g' is followed by the vowels 'e', 'i' or 'y' it makes the sound 'j' like in 'jam' and is called a 'soft g' sound. Now you will learn to read and spell words with the soft g sound.

Use this QR code to watch and listen to the **letter G** sound cards below

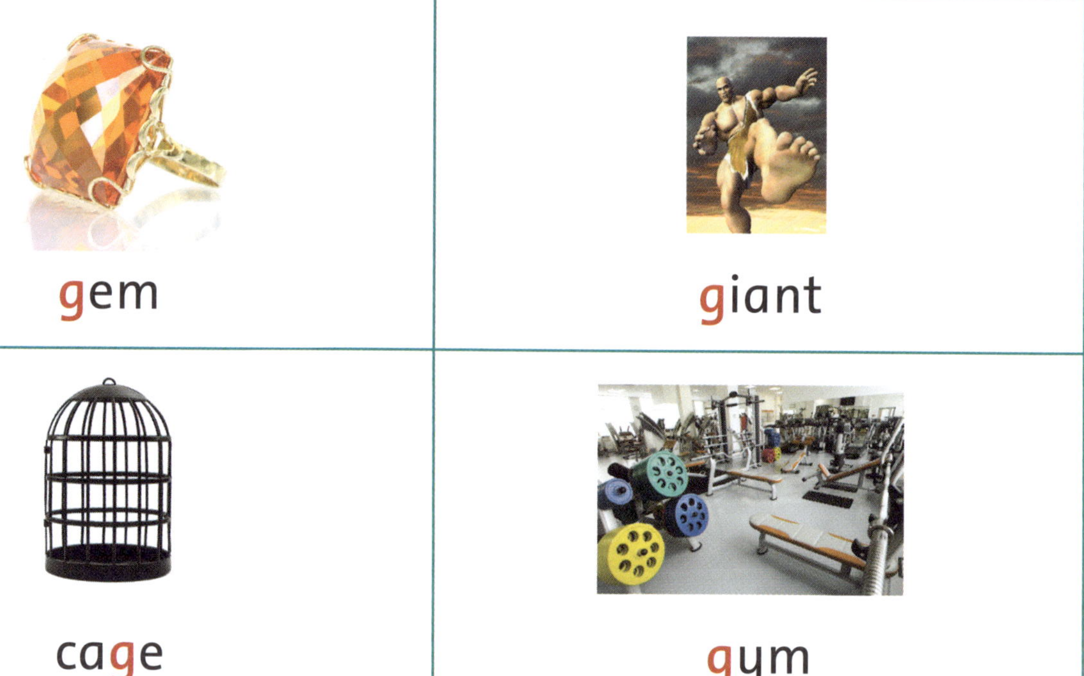

Kimba kangaroo knows some rockslide words have soft g. Colour them for him.

  ISBN: 9781925726350

Consonant sound j with the soft g as in *gem*

Say the names of the pictures. Listen for the 'soft g' sound. Write the word below. Remember to write the e on the end if you need it.

Handwriting

Trace the words then copy them onto the lines below.

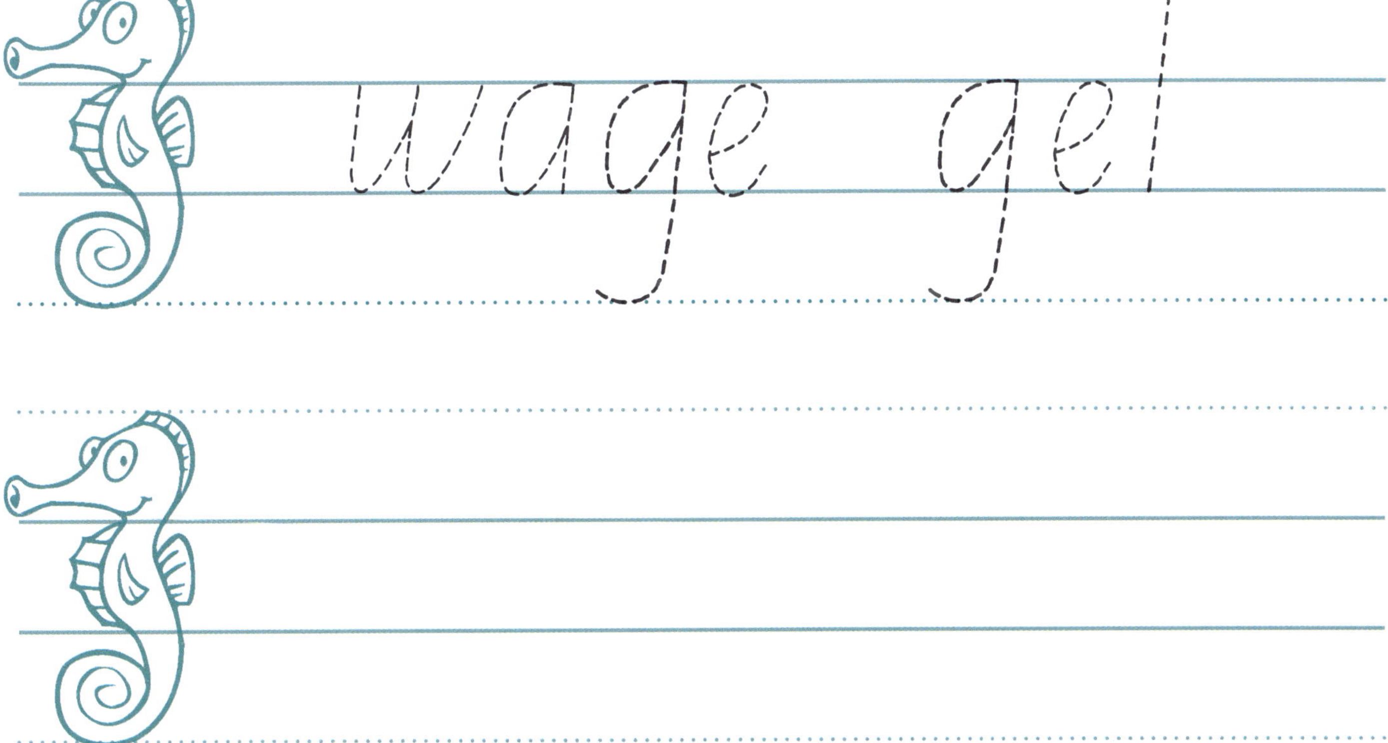

  ISBN: 9781925726350

⋆ Unit 5 Review ⋆

Consonant sounds 'soft c' and 'soft g', and long vowel sounds 'oo' as in flute, moon, screw.
Read the words. Draw lines to match them to the pictures.

Spelling

Say the names of the pictures below. Write the letters that are missing from each word.

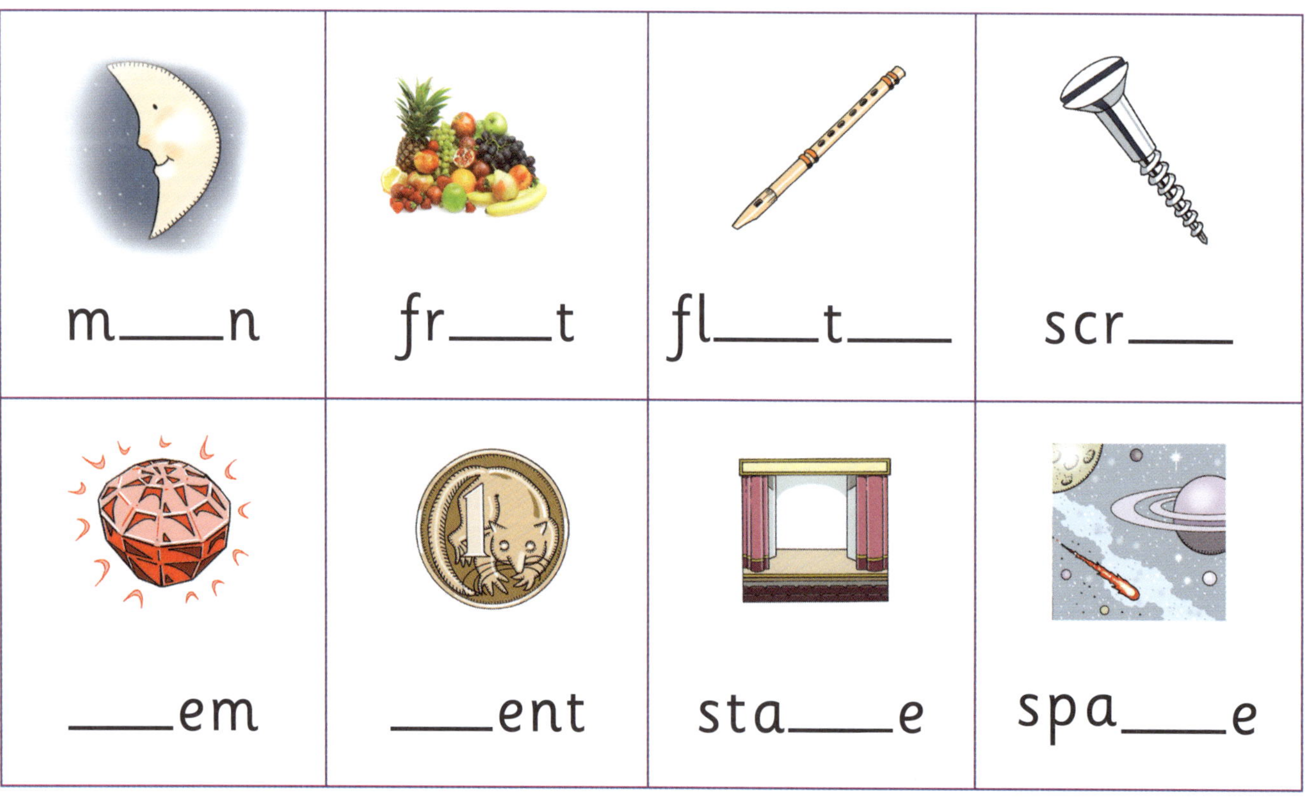

  ISBN: 9781925726350

Long vowel sounds *oo*

There are different ways to spell the long *oo* sound as in *moon*.
Decode to read these words.

Read and draw

Finish the words with u_e, oo, ew, ui or ue. Then draw a picture of the word you made.

sp__n	fr__t	gl__
scr__	fl__t__	b__t

Choose the correct word

Consonant sounds 'soft c' and 'soft g' and long 'oo' sound. Look at the pictures. Read the pairs of words. Circle the correct word.

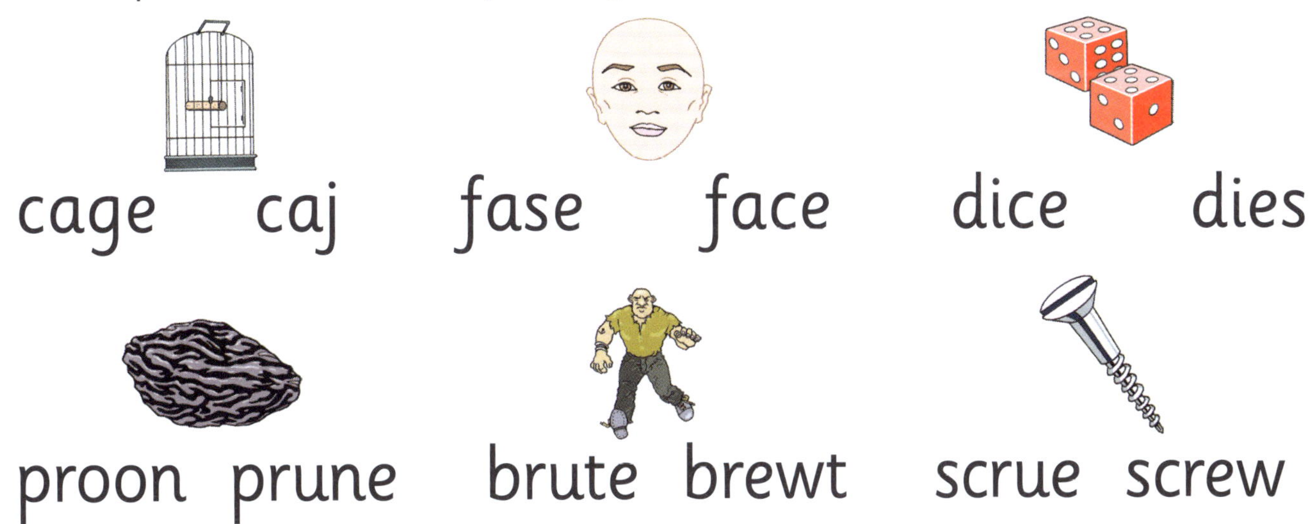

  ISBN: 9781925726350

⋆ Consonant sounds soft c and soft g and long oo sound ⋆

Decoding

Now you know these letters and sounds. You can blend them to make and read these words. Remember to use the soft c and the soft g in the first five words.

Say the sounds	Blend the sounds	Read the word
Point to each letter as you say the sound.	Slide your finger from one sound to the next as you say the sound.	Point to the word as you read it.
c e n t	c e n t	cent
g e l	g e l	gel
c a g e	c a g	cage
f a c e	f a c	face
j ui c e	j ui c	juice
s p oo n	s p oo n	spoon
ch ew	ch ew	chew
g l ue	g l ue	glue
f r ui t	f r ui e t	fruit
z oo m	z oo m	zoom

Spelling

Say the names of the pictures below. Stretch out the word to hear the sound at the beginning, the sound in the middle and the sound at the end. Write the words on the lines below. Don't forget the 'e' on the end if you need it.

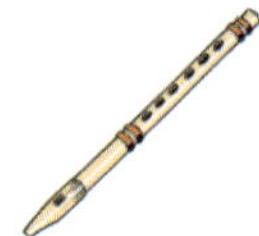

  ISBN: 9781925726350

Handwriting

Now you can read these words, you can write them too.

Trace the words. Then write them on the lines below.

brute face roof

nice threw pool

cage zoo fruit

  ISBN: 9781925726350

High frequency words – Unit 5

Here are some high frequency words to learn by sight.

can't	new	our	friend	school

Comprehension

Read the sentences. Draw a picture to match.

We went to the pool. We went on our new school bus. We had some juice and some food to eat. It was fun.	I went to the zoo with my friend. We saw a huge moose. It was in a big cage. It likes to eat fruit. It can't eat meat.

I like to play games with my sister. We play with a dice. We get five cents when we throw a six. My sister threw a six twice in a row. She got ten cents.	A little plant grew by our pool. "That plant can't grow here," said Dad. He put it in a pot. "You can grow here, little plant," said Dad.

  ISBN: 9781925726350

Comprehension

Look at the pictures. Read the sentences. Write in the missing word.

The little girl made a ship to go up into

__ __ __ __ __.

Dad put on his

__ __ __ __ __.

Then he went to get some food for lunch.

I saw a

__ __ __ __ __

chew some fruit at the zoo.

This sentence is jumbled. Write it correctly on the lines below.

The is in sky. moon the bright

  ISBN: 9781925726350

Consonant sound z spelt with s as in *nose*

You already know that the letter 's' is used to spell words such as snake, sun, and sand. You also know that the letter 'z' is used to spell words like zoo, zoom and zip. Now you will learn that sometimes the letter 's' makes the sound 'z' as in nose, rose and logs. It makes the 'z' sound when it follows a vowel or a voiced consonant.

Use this QR code to watch and listen to the **letter S** sound cards below

Colour the road signs bright red if they have a z sound.

Consonant sound z when spelt with s as in *nose*

Say the names of the pictures. Write the word below.
Remember to write the letter 's' although you hear the 'z' sound.

Handwriting

Trace the words then copy them onto the lines below.

  ISBN: 9781925726350

Short vowel sound  with the digraph oo as in *book*

Use this QR code to watch and listen to the **letter OO** sound cards below

 book	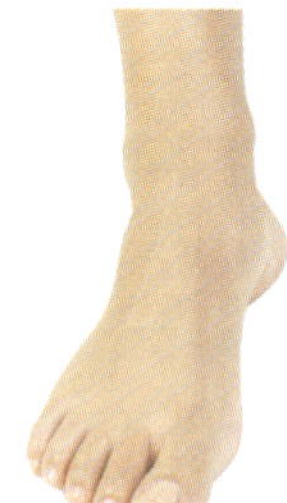 foot
 wood	 wool

Can you find all the short **oo** sounds and colour the pictures?

Short vowel sound oo with the digraph oo as in *book*

Say the names of the pictures. Listen for the 'oo' sound.
Write the word below.

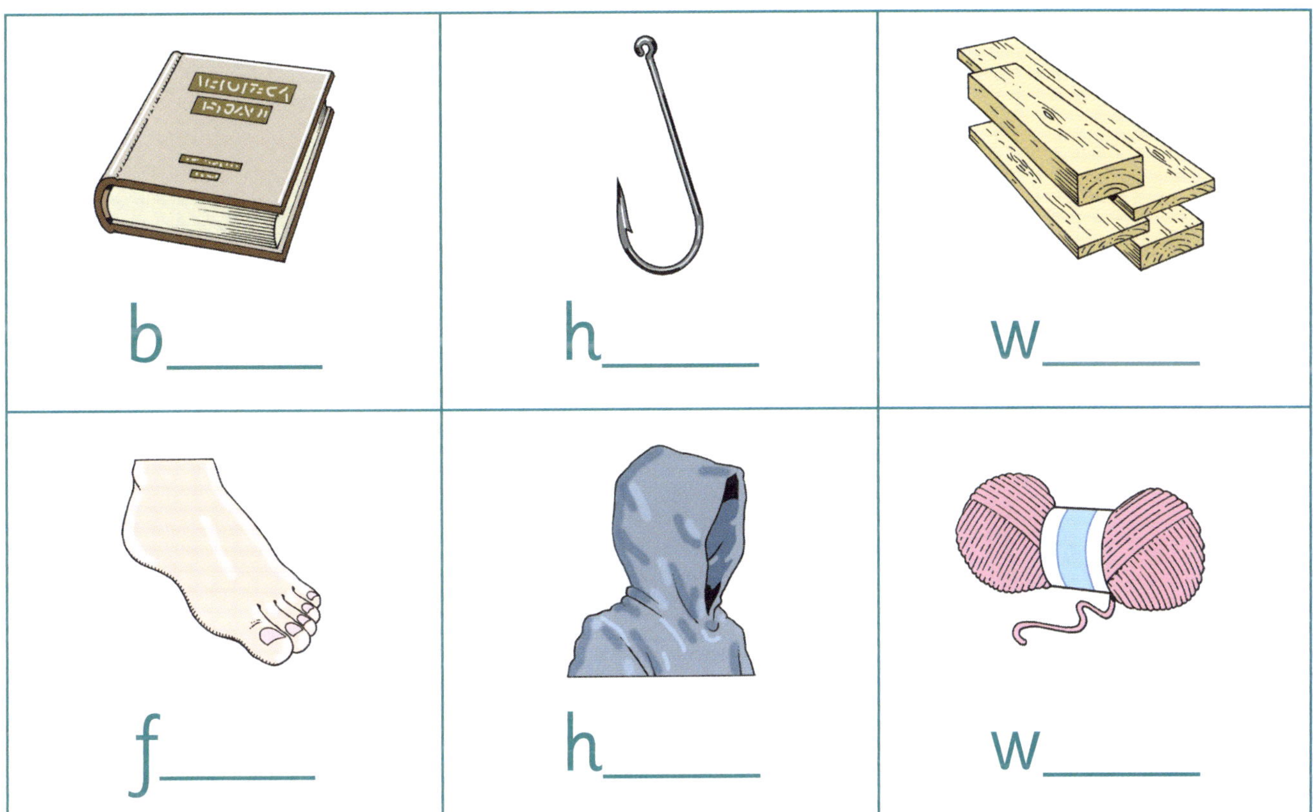

Handwriting

Trace the words then copy them onto the lines below.

 © PASCAL PRESS ISBN: 9781925726350

More about the letter 

You already know that the letter 's' is used to spell words such as snake, sun, and sand. You also know that the letter 's' is used to spell works like nose, rose and logs. You know that when it is with 'h' it forms a digraph and makes 'sh' as in ship, shop and show. It also makes the 'sh' sound when it's on its own, like in sugar.Let's practice words with 's'.

Use this QR code to watch and listen to the **letter S** sound cards below

Find the words with the **s**, **sh** or **z** sounds and write the sound in the circle next to them.

  ISBN: 9781925726350

More about the letter s

Say the names of the pictures. Draw lines to match the words to the sounds you hear.

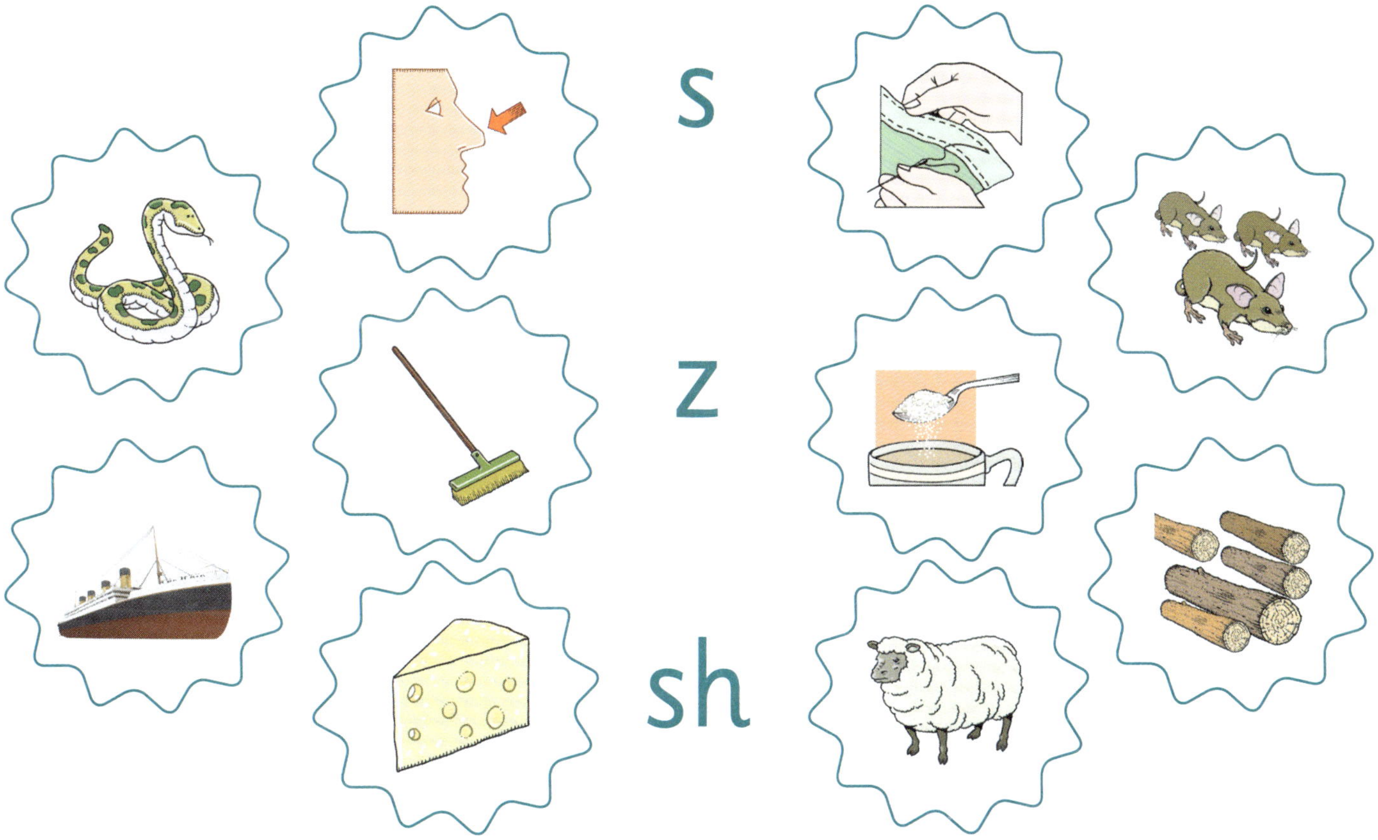

s

z

sh

Handwriting

Trace the words then copy them onto the lines below.

  ISBN: 9781925726350

Long vowel sound oo as in *moon* and short vowel sound oo as in *book*

You already know that the letters 'oo' are used to spell words such as moon, pool and food. You also know that the letters 'oo' are used to spell words like book, wood and foot. Now you will learn other ways to spell the short vowel 'oo' as in book.

Use this QR code to watch and listen to the **letter OO** sound cards below

 bull	 bush
 puss	 full

Have a hoot by adding colour to all of the words with a long **oo** sound like **moon**.

  ISBN: 9781925726350

Long vowel sound oo as in *moon* and short vowel sound oo as in *book*

Say the names of the pictures. Draw lines to match the words to the sounds you hear.

oo
as in
moon

oo
as in
book

Handwriting

Trace the words then copy them onto the lines below.

These words also have the short vowel sound 'oo'.

put	could
push	should
pull	would

blew pull

  ISBN: 9781925726350

⋆ Unit 6 Review ⋆

Consonant ‘s’ and vowel sounds ‘oo’ as in book

Read the words. Draw lines to match them to the pictures.

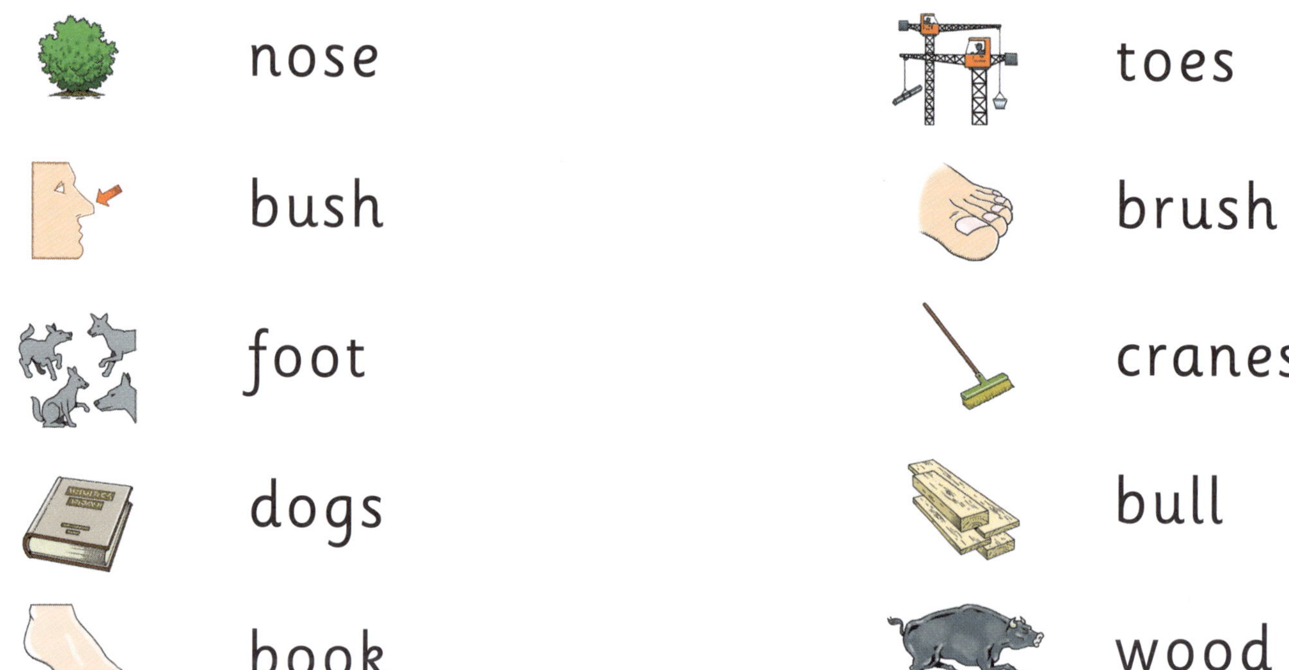

Spelling

Say the names of the pictures below. Write the letters that are missing from each word.

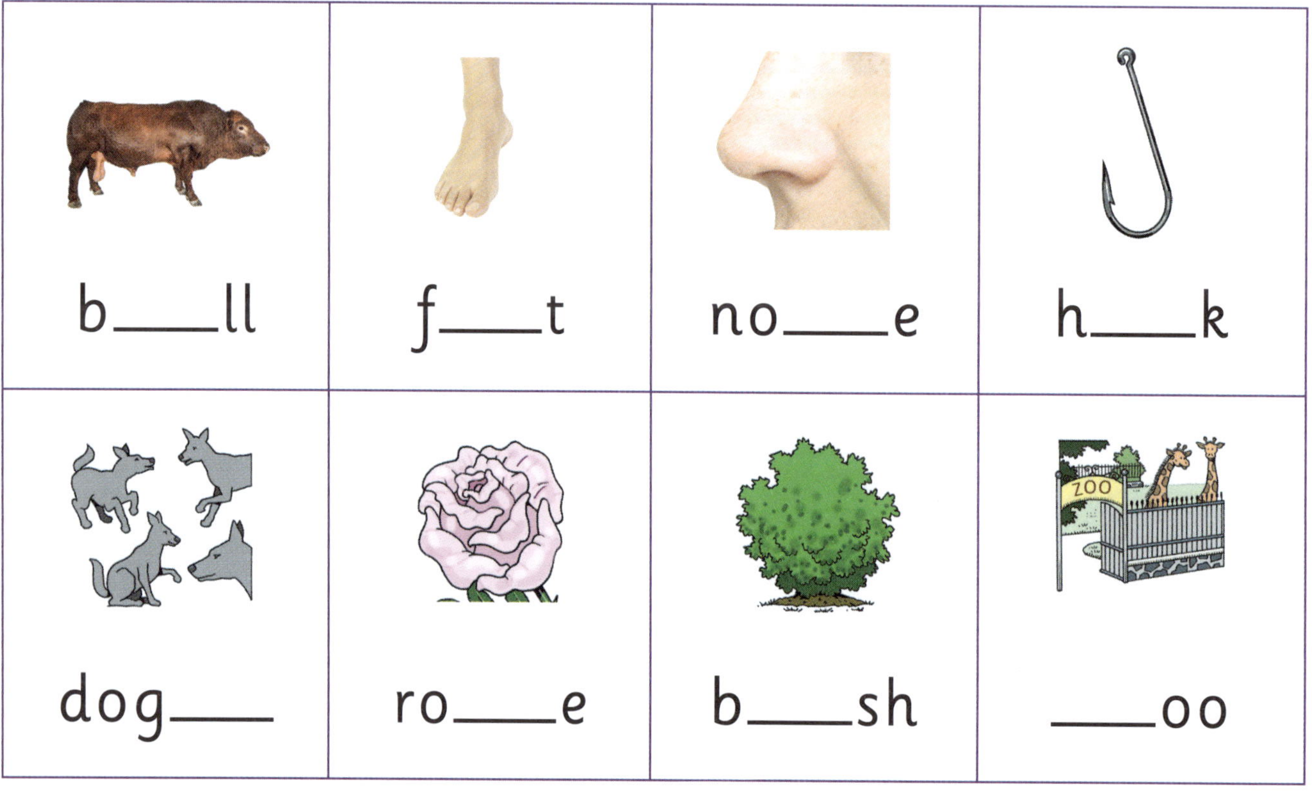

  ISBN: 9781925726350

Long vowel sound oo as in *moon* and short vowel sound oo as in *book*

Say the names of the pictures. Draw lines to match the words to the sounds you hear.

Read and draw

Finish the words with oo or u. Then draw a picture of the word you made.

h___k	b___ll	b___k
w___d	b___sh	f___t

Choose the correct word

Look at the pictures. Read the pairs of words.
Circle the correct word.

full fool

dogs dog

push pull

  ISBN: 9781925726350

★ Consonant s and vowel sounds oo as in *book* ★

Decoding

Now you know these letters and sounds. You can blend them to make and read these words.

Say the sounds	Blend the sounds	Read the word
Point to each letter as you say the sound.	Slide your finger from one sound to the next as you say the sound.	Point to the word as you read it.
n o s e	n o s	nose
l o g s	l o g s	logs
h e n s	h e n s	hens
w oo d s	w oo d s	woods
l oo k	l oo k	look
ch oo k	ch oo k	chook
f u ll	f u ll	full
b u sh	b u sh	bush
g oo d	g oo d	good
c oul d	c oul d	could

Spelling

Say the names of the pictures below. Stretch out the word to hear the sound at the beginning, the sound in the middle and the sound at the end. Write the words on the lines below.

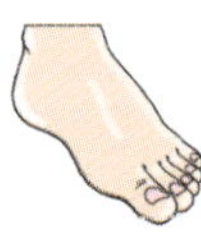

  ISBN: 9781925726350

Handwriting

Now you can read these words, you can write them too.
Trace the words. Then write them on the lines below.

nose cranes brook

push pull foot

could would should

High frequency words – Unit 6

Here are some high frequency words to learn by sight.

near	goes	could	should	would

Comprehension

Read the sentences. Draw a picture to match.

A girl put a rose near her nose. A bee was in the rose. The bee did not sting her nose. The bee gave her a fright. "You should not put your nose in a rose," her brother said.	"You should cook the cakes on these trays," said Mum. "I could cook the cakes on these trays," I said. "But I would like to cook them on those trays."

The man has an axe. The man will use his axe to chop wood. He will cut some logs from the wood.	My brother would like to play a game. I would like to read my book. What should I do? Will I read my book? No. I will play games with my brother.

  ISBN: 9781925726350

Comprehension

Look at the pictures. Read the sentences. Write in the missing word.

A lot of bees fly near the rose __ __ __ __.

The boys and girls play games with their pet __ __ __ __.

We read our __ __ __ __ __ near the tree after lunch.

This sentence is jumbled. Write it correctly on the lines below.

cakes the The trays. cook on put the

  ISBN: 9781925726350

★ Book 2 Revision ★

Decoding

Read the words. Draw lines to match them to the pictures.

cane

bike

ship

dish

cheese

mole

cube

moth

snail

eight

swing

pie

wheel

spoon

cage

  ISBN: 9781925726350

Spelling

Say the names of the pictures below. Stretch out the word to hear the sound at the beginning, the sound in the middle and the sound at the end. Write the words on the lines below.

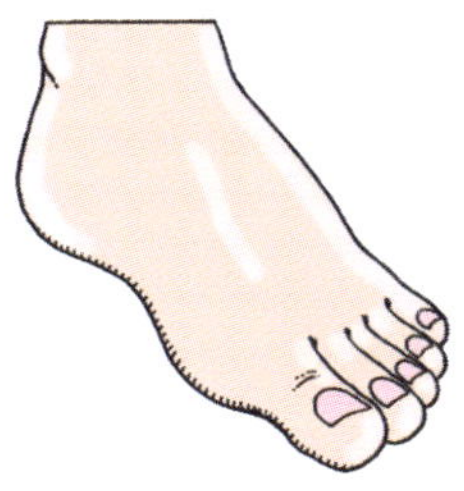

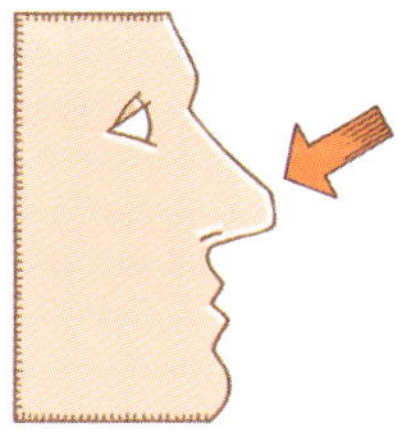

  ISBN: 9781925726350

Rhyming words

Use letters you know to write words that rhyme with the pictured words. Be careful. Different letters can be used to spell the same sound.

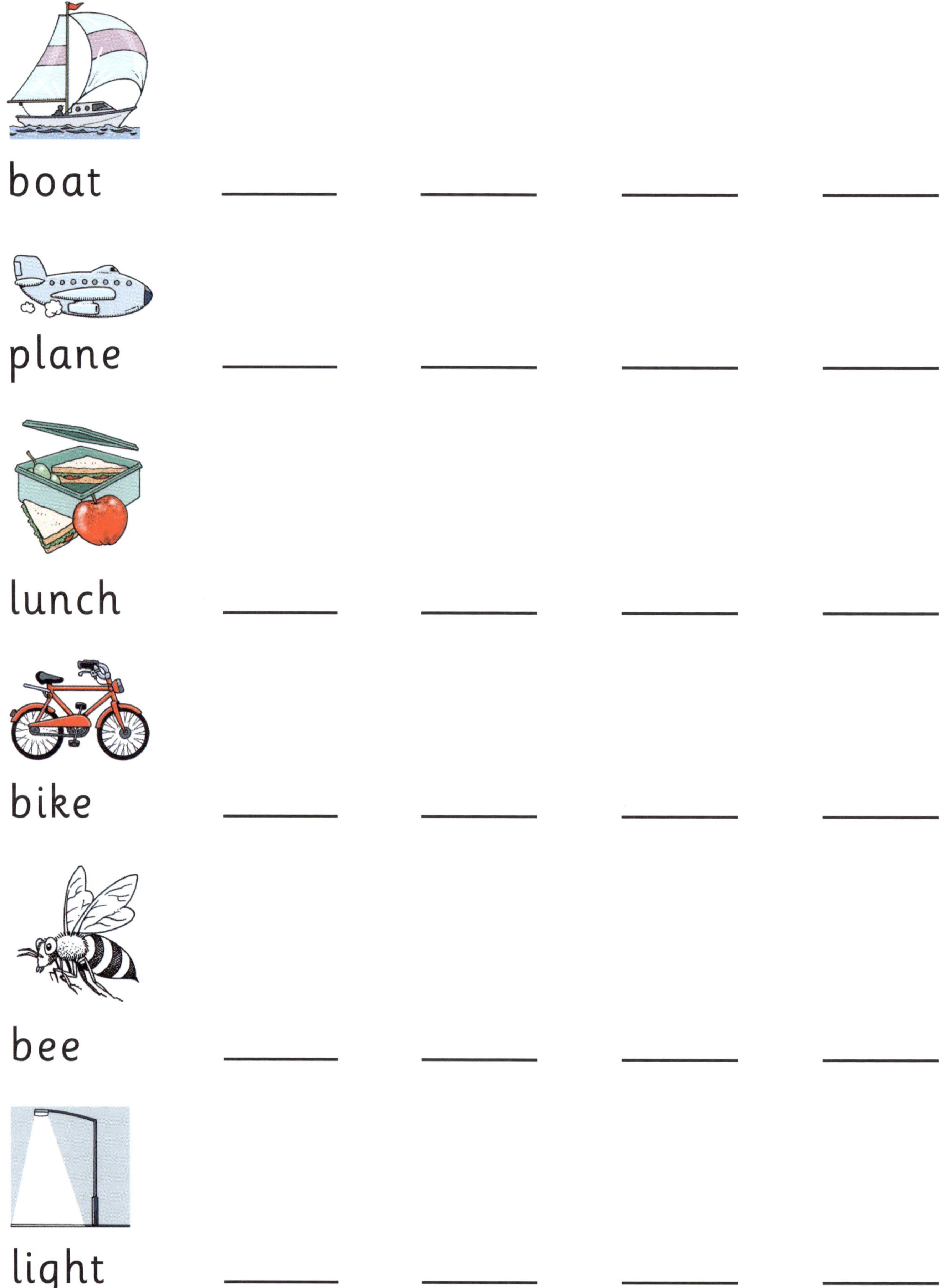

  ISBN: 9781925726350

Comprehension

Read the sentences. Draw a picture to match.

The brother and sister are twins. They made a new friend at school. They like to race with their friend at lunch time.	We play a game with dice in maths. We throw six dice. Then we add the dots. If you threw the most, you win.

We went to the zoo with Mum and Dad. We went on the train. We saw a yak. We saw a sloth. We saw a quoll. We saw a fox and we saw a skunk. It was fun at the zoo.	When we went to camp, we took some food for lunch. We took a loaf of bread, some meat, some fruit and some juice to drink.

  ISBN: 9781925726350

Comprehension

Read the sentences. Write in the missing word.

When the boy fell into the __ __ __ __, he made a big splash.

My dog likes to __ __ __ __ my dad's boot.

My sister looks at cakes in her cook __ __ __ __. She will bake a cake.

This sentence is jumbled. Write it correctly on the lines below.

high. can The lift crane wood the up

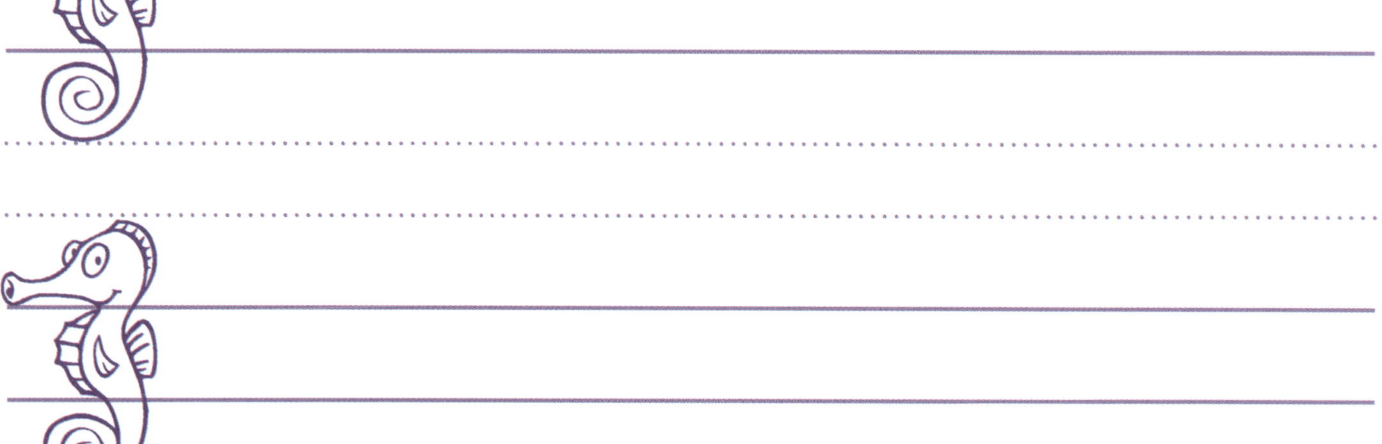

⋆A Selection of Decodable Words⋆

UNIT 1 A_E, I_E, SH, CH

cake	make	made	wave	tape
dale	male	sale	tale	lane
tame	same	name	fame	mane
cane	cape	case	base	taste
line	like	pine	pike	ride
bike	tribe	ripe	pride	hide
life	tile	file	time	crime
lime	dine	wipe	bite	kite
ship	shop	shot	shape	shame

  ISBN: 9781925726350

shut	shin	shine	shade	shun
wish	dish	fish	bash	crash
gosh	posh	mesh	mush	crush
chip	chop	chap	chime	chafe
chat	champ	chase	chick	chess
rich	lunch	bench	such	much
pinch	crunch	munch	bunch	hunch

  ISBN: 9781925726350

robe	lobe	probe	rode	node
role	dole	hole	mole	pole
sole	dome	home	hope	rope
note	lone	tone	stone	rote
mule	cute	cube	tube	dune
fume	tune	dupe	mute	
that	than	this	then	them
thine	thus	clothe	bathe	lathe
thin	think	thank	thick	thud
cloth	broth	with	moth	sloth

  ISBN: 9781925726350

rain	hail	pail	mail	train
snail	main	plain	paid	maid
pay	day	may	say	tray
ray	pray	stay	hay	play
eight	weight	freight	neigh	sleigh
bee	sheep	cheep	feet	teeth
seed	need	green	keep	deep
bean	beach	bead	peach	teach
reach	sea	eat	read	seal
phone				

  ISBN: 9781925726350

UNIT 3 PH, NG, LONG A, LONG E

thong	sing	song	king	ring
long	bang	sang	rang	bring
strong	swing	clang	rung	hang

UNIT 4 WH, C/K, LONG I, LONG O

pie	die	lie	tie	tied
by	cry	try	fry	dry
shy	my	spy	sky	fly
high	sigh	nigh	fight	light
right	night	sight	bright	might
whale	white	when	wheel	whip

  ISBN: 9781925726350

whisk	wheat	which	why	while
boat	road	coat	float	soap
coach	coal	loaf	toast	toad
toe	hoe	doe	foe	floe
so	no	go	bow	slow
blow	tow	sow	flow	show
low	tow	row	mow	stow
bowl				

  ISBN: 9781925726350

dude	rule	rude	rune	prune
prude	flute	brute	June	flume
cent	cell	place	space	spice
dice	twice	nice	face	ace
moon	spoon	food	boot	roof
fruit	suit	juice	pool	moose
drew	flew	threw	brew	crew
screw	chew	shrew	grew	clue
blue	glue	flue	true	sue
zoo	too	boo	moo	zoom
gem	cage	huge	rage	page
wage	age	gel	stage	

  ISBN: 9781925726350

nose	rose	pose	toes	goes
logs	dogs	games	cranes	trays
fries	tries	lies	pies	dies
book	foot	wood	wool	good
cook	look	hook	chook	brook
pull	push	bush	bull	full
put	could	would	should	

  ISBN: 9781925726350

★ High Frequency Words — Unit 1 ★

your	day	play	his	her
all	their	after	she	came

★ High Frequency Words — Unit 2 ★

walk	by	be	stay	water
brother	sister	out	please	saw

★ High Frequency Words — Unit 3 ★

as	put

★ High Frequency Words — Unit 4 ★

who	whole	what	guy	buy

★ High Frequency Words — Unit 5 ★

can't	new	our	friend	school

★ High Frequency Words — Unit 6 ★

near	goes	could	should	would

ANSWERS
Review and Assessment Sections

Please note that answers may vary slightly for some questions.

BOOK 1 REVIEW

Page 11	hand, cat, doll, red; Dan and Sam went in a black van.

UNIT 1

Page 13	gate, snake, plane, cage, lake, game.
Page 15	shell, fish, shed, brush, crash, shop.
Page 17	five, nine, smile, bride, hive, pipe.
Page 19	chin, chick, chess, chop, lunch, bench.

UNIT 1 REVIEW

Page 20	ship, chip, cake, kite, bike, shop, chop, gate
Page 21	cake, snake, gate, kite, bike, pipe; cane, ship, chop, bike, kite, bunch
Page 22	plane, shell, chop, lunch, bike, fish
Page 25	cake, fish, chips, bike; We had fish and chips for lunch.

UNIT 2

Page 27	mole, dome, pole, home, hole, rope.
Page 29	father, fish, feather, mother, there.
Page 31	mule, cute, tune, dune, cube, tube.
Page 33	thin, thick, moth, throne, think, cloth.

UNIT 2 REVIEW

Page 34	think, thin, home, mule, cube, moth, brother, rope
Page 35	mole, home, rope, mule, tube, cube; mole, cub, thin, broth, moth, think

  ISBN: 9781925726350

Page 36	mule, mole, think, moth, broth, cube
Page 39	cube, hole, mule; I have a brother and a sister at home.

UNIT 3

Page 41	train, tail, rain, play, day, hay.
Page 43	phone, dolphin, elephant, photo, sphere, graph
Page 45	bee, feet, teeth, beach, bean, jeans.
Page 47	ring, wing, sing, swing, king, fang

UNIT 3 REVIEW

Page 48	phone, sheep, snail, hay, beach, ring, sing, bean
Page 49	snake, day, train, hay, bake, rain; tree, me, beach, seal, green, leaf
Page 50	plane, snail, phone, king, beach, sheep
Page 53	king, phone, rock; Dad will hang a swing for us to play.

UNIT 4

Page 55	pie, spy, tie, night, fight, light.
Page 56	whale, wheel, white, whisk, wheat, whip.
Page 59	boat, toad, soap, toe, doe, hoe.
Page 61	cup, king, duck, kite, cake, chick.

UNIT 4 REVIEW

Page 62	goat, pie, night, sky, bow, can, kite, truck
Page 63	tie, night, fly, spy, bike, pie; hoe, boat, soap, bow, home, loaf
Page 64	pie, fight, whale, loaf, truck, cap
Page 67	plane, boat, whale; I like to eat my toast with jam.

  ISBN: 9781925726350

UNIT 5

Page 69	flute, brute, prune, cube, mule, tune.
Page 71	ice, face, dice, mice, cent, space.
Page 73	moon, spoon, boot, crew, chew, screw.
Page 75	gem, gel, cage, stage, huge, page.

UNIT 5 REVIEW

Page 76	moon, fruit, flute, screw, gem, cent, stage, space
Page 77	spoon, fruit, glue, screw, flute, boot; cage, face, dice, prune, brute, screw
Page 78	flute, space, cent, cage, moose, glue
Page 81	space, boots, moose; The moon is bright in the sky.

UNIT 6

Page 83	nose, toes, fries, dogs, rose, hands.
Page 85	book, hook, wood, foot, hood, wool.
Page 90	bull, foot, nose, hook, dogs, rose, bush, zoo.

UNIT 6 REVIEW

Page 91	hook, bull, book, wood, bush, foot; full, dogs, push
Page 92	book, bush, full, foot, cook, bull
Page 95	bush, dogs, books; The cook put the cakes on the trays.

ASSESSMENT

Page 97	boot, foot, nose, juice, bow, coat
Page 98	answers will vary but can include; goat, train, crunch, like, see, night
Page 100	pool, chew, book; The crane can lift the wood up high.

  ISBN: 9781925726350